LEGAL RESEARCH GUIDES

VOLUME 37

ISRAEL:
A LEGAL RESEARCH GUIDE

ISRAEL:
A LEGAL RESEARCH GUIDE

By

Esther M. Snyder
Bar-Ilan University
Director, Law Faculty Library

William S. Hein & Co., Inc.
Buffalo, New York
2000

Library of Congress Cataloging-in-Publication Data

Snyder, Esther M.

Israel : a legal research guide / by Esther M. Snyder.
p. cm. — (Legal research guides ; v. 37)

Includes bibliographical references.

ISBN 1-57588-528-X (cloth : alk. paper)

1. Legal research—Israel. I. Title. II. Series.

KMK47 .S65 2000
340'.07'25694—dc21 00-033603

Printed in the United States of America

This volume is printed on acid-free paper by
William S. Hein & Co., Inc.

LEGAL RESEARCH GUIDES

Volume 1
RESEARCH GUIDE TO PROFESSIONAL CORPORATE LAW
Peter Aitelli & Debra M. Dietrich

Volume 2
COVERING ALL THE BASES:
A COMPREHENSIVE RESEARCH GUIDE TO SPORTS LAW
2nd Edition
Gary A. Uberstine

Volume 3
WOMEN, SPORTS AND THE LAW:
A COMPREHENSIVE RESEARCH GUIDE
TO SEX DISCRIMINATION IN SPORTS
Karen Tokarz

Volume 4
TEENAGE PREGNANCY:
A RESEARCH GUIDE TO PROGRAMS AND SERVICES
Patrice A. Gillotti

Volume 5
THE AUTOMATED TELLER MACHINE (ATM)
AS A NATIONAL BANK "BRANCH" UNDER FEDERAL LAW
Kirk Peterson

Volume 6
RESEARCH GUIDE:
SURROGATE MOTHERHOOD
Kathleen K. Bach

Volume 7
A PRACTITIONER'S GUIDE TO
JOINT PHYSICAL CUSTODY OF CHILDREN
Michelle Virzi

Volume 8
CIVIL RICO: A RESEARCH GUIDE TO
CIVIL LIABILITY FOR BUSINESS CRIMES
Peter Somers Dickinson

Volume 9
CGL INSURANCE COVERAGE FOR
CLEAN UP OF HAZARDOUS SUBSTANCES
Emily M. Defalla

Volume 10
PRIVATE SECTOR FEDERAL EMPLOYMENT DISCRIMINATION
Luke Farber

Volume 11
AUTOMATED TELLER MACHINE CRIME:
ARE BANKS LIABLE FOR PERSONAL INJURIES?
Pamela Samuels

Volume 12
BLOCKADE LAW:
RESEARCH DESIGN AND SOURCES
Michael N. Schmitt

Volume 13
RESOURCES FOR RESEARCH IN LEGAL ETHICS
Todd W. Grant

Volume 14
MERGERS AND THE FEDERAL ANTITRUST LAWS:
A RESEARCH GUIDE FOR PRACTITIONERS
Perry Goldberg

Volume 15
EQUAL EDUCATION OPPORTUNITY FOR ALL CHILDREN:
A RESEARCH GUIDE TO DISCRIMINATION IN EDUCATION (1950–1992)
Deborah Mayo-Jefferies

Volume 16
RELIGIOUS FREEDOM IN THE EDUCATION PROCESS:
A RESEARCH GUIDE TO RELIGION IN EDUCATION (1950–1992)
Deborah Mayo-Jefferies

Volume 17
LIMITED LIABILITY COMPANIES
Mary Virginia Moore

Volume 18
A PATHFINDER TO
U.S. EXPORT CONTROL LAWS AND REGULATIONS
Wei Luo

Volume 19
LEGAL RESEARCH IN LAW FIRMS
Terry C. M. Hutchinson

Volume 20
A GUIDE TO RESEARCHING THE CHILD CARE COMPONENT OF THE FAMILY SUPPORT ACT OF 1988
Ingrid V. Eagly

Volume 21
LEGAL RESEARCH GUIDE TO MECHANICAL PATENT LITIGATION
Adam V. Floyd

Volume 22
LEGAL RESEARCH GUIDE TO TELEVISION BROADCASTING AND PROGRAM SYNDICATION
Teresa A. Lee

Volume 23
EDUCATIONAL MALPRACTICE: A PATHFINDER
Sharon L. Lockhart

Volume 24
LEGAL MALPRACTICE: A RESEARCH GUIDE FOR LAWYERS AND LAW STUDENTS
Patrick G. Reavey

Volume 25
REPRODUCTIVE TECHNOLOGY: A RESEARCH GUIDE TO THE LEGAL STATUS OF THE FROZEN HUMAN EMBRYO
Timothy Coppo

Volume 26
DEATH ON DEMAND: PHYSICIAN-ASSISTED SUICIDE IN THE UNITED STATES: A LEGAL RESEARCH PATHFINDER
Cathleen DeSimone

Volume 27
LEGAL RESEARCH GUIDE TO POST-TRAUMATIC STRESS DISORDER
Steven R. Thorpe

Volume 28
PATHFINDERS OF THE TEXAS STATE LAW LIBRARY

Volume 29
A GUIDE TO RESEARCHING THE INTERNATIONAL PRINCIPLE OF SELF-DETERMINATION
Michael Mosberg

Volume 30
EMPLOYMENT DISCRIMINATION
BASED ON SEXUAL ORIENTATION
Gabriel M. Nugent

Volume 31
A LEGAL RESEARCH GUIDE TO
AMERICAN THOROUGHBRED RACING LAW FOR
SCHOLARS, PRACTITIONERS AND PARTICIPANTS
Joan S. Howland
Michael J. Hannon

Volume 32
LEGAL RESEARCH GUIDES OF
TEXAS TECH UNIVERSITY
Douglas W. Gardner
Wesley T. D. Myers

Volume 33
LEGAL RESEARCH ON THE INTERNET
Antje Mays

Volume 34
AIDS, EXPERIMENTAL DRUG APPROVAL,
AND THE FDA NEW DRUG SCREENING PROCESS:
A LEGAL RESEARCH GUIDE
Michael D. Greenberg

Volume 35
EMPLOYMENT COMPLIANCE REQUIREMENTS UNDER THE
AMERICANS WITH DISABILITIES ACT FOR THE MENTALLY ILL
EMPLOYEE AND POTENTIAL APPLICANT: A PATHFINDER
E. Laurita Finch

Volume 36
THE PRESERVATION AND PROTECTION OF
AMERICA'S CULTURAL RESOURCES:
A LEGAL RESEARCH GUIDE
Jenny Hodgkins

TABLE OF CONTENTS

PREFACE

This work is a survey of the bibliographic sources of the law in Israel. It is intended for the law researcher, lawyer and information specialist/ librarian who seek to discover and use Israel legal materials. In addition, some basic, relevant background information is given for the Israel legal system, the legislature and the courts. The opening chapters deal with the **Primary Sources—legislation, subsidiary legislation and judicial decisions**—while the following chapters cover the **secondary materials—periodicals** and **collections of essays** and **reference books;** later sections discuss the new, electronic formats—**CD-Roms** and **Internet Websites.** Chapters on **Jewish Law** and **Pre-State materials** complete the survey.

Two **pathfinders** appear to facilitate finding statutes (p.12) and cases (p.26). Other tips and advice are given stemming from the experience of almost 30 years as a law librarian in Israel.

The **Appendices** have additional material which should prove useful to the researcher and the reference librarian and they include: a**List of Justices of the Supreme Court and Presidents of the State,** a **Selected Bibliography of Books and Articles in English**—this is a comprehensive list of important works arranged by subject; a **List of Abbreviations**—a reprint of the list which appears in the **World Dictionary of Legal Abbreviations,** and **the Declaration of the Establishment of the State and Proclamation.**

As most of the materials are in Hebrew, transliterations have been used and translations given where necessary. The Hebrew letter "het" has been transliterated as "h", while the Hebrew letter "kaf" appears as "kh".

Thanks and appreciation are hereby extended to the staff of the Law Library of Bar-Ilan University who were both supportive and helpful in preparing this work: Batya Razinski for the chapters on primary sources, Lia Levy for the chapters on CD-Roms and Websites, and Hedva Shem-Tov for preparing the lists of justices and presidents. Hilda Schmerler, librarian emeritus, excelled in typing and editing most of the manuscript.

The chapter on Jewish Law was improved by the suggestions of Prof. Arnold Enker of the Law Faculty.

Some sections are similar in content to those that appeared in an article of mine which appeared in 70 Law Library Journal 14 (1977); this book, however, is a new, completely reworked, revised, enlarged and updated publication.

Finally, I'd like to dedicate this book to my wonderful daughters, Lea and Sharona, and to my sweet granddaughter, Nili.

E.M. Snyder
January 2000

CHAPTER 1 : ISRAEL LEGAL SYSTEM

The State of Israel is a representative parliamentary democracy, where the government functions as the executive branch and is headed by the Prime Minister and other ministers appointed by him usually as part of a coalition government.[1] The Knesset, Israel's parliament, constitutes the legislative branch.[2] Its 120 members are elected via political party lists in direct, proportional elections which are held every four years or sooner if the government fails to win a vote of confidence or resigns . The President of the State [3] is elected by the Knesset and his powers are mainly of a representative character although he also has one important role in entrusting the task of forming a government to one of the members of the Knesset, after consulting with the party factions. However, after the enactment of the direct election of prime minister, the President no longer has this function. [4] The court system, headed by the Supreme Court, constitutes the judicial branch.[5]

The laws of the legal system consist of several distinct elements; in addition to the acts passed by the Knesset and the judicial precedents of the courts since the establishment of the state in 1948, the body of law includes remnants of previous foreign administrations.

With independence the new state kept intact much of the existing rules and regulations from the Mandate administration but also initiated new legislation in areas of law not otherwise regulated. Many acts have been passed in the field of private law while public law has been developed mainly through judicial decisions. In addition to some Turkish influences (Palestine was part of the Ottoman Empire from 1517 to 1917) and English common law principles (inherited from the British Mandate, 1922-1948), there are also clear and important influences from the American legal system due to the close relations between the two countries and their citizens.

Another important element is that of Jewish law. The Foundations of Law Act was passed in 1980 and its purpose is to encourage the use of traditional Jewish sources . When there is no statute law or case law on a particular subject, the law states that the court should decide "in the light

---

1 Basic Law: The Government (1992)

2 Basic Law: The Knesset, 12 L.S.I. 85 (1958)

3 Basic law: President of the State, 18 L.S.I. 111 (1964)

4 For a comprehensive survey see A.Maoz, "The institutional organization of the Israeli legal system", Introduction to the Law of Israel, ed. A.Shapira (Kluwer, 1995)

5 Basic Law: Judicature, 38 L.S.I. 101 (1984); Courts Law (Consolidated Version), 1984

of the principles of freedom, justice, equity and peace of Israel's heritage".[6] For more on this subject see the chapter on Jewish Law.

Thus the Israel legal system is a unique synthesis of continental or civil law (from the Ottomans), common law (British), original Israeli legislative acts and elements of Jewish law.

HISTORICAL BACKGROUND

The State of Israel, which may be considered the third Jewish Commonwealth in the Land of Israel (Palestine), was established on May 14, 1948. The first Jewish Commonwealth , begun more than 2500 years ago ended in 586 B.C.E. (before the Common Era) with the destruction of the holy Temple by the Babylonians. The conquest of Jerusalem by the Roman forces in 70 C.E. (Common Era) marked the end of the second commonwealth.

The Land of Israel was part of the Roman and Byzantine empires until 633 when the Moslems entered Palestine where they ruled almost six hundred years. The Ottoman Turks conquered Palestine and Egypt in 1517; Palestine remained under Turkish rule for four hundred years until their defeat in World War I .

The local law in Turkey and in the whole Ottoman Empire was made up of codes, most notably the Mejelle which is an all-encompassing civil code based on Islamic legal principles. Other codes were "borrowed" from or influenced by France, as for instance, the Napoleanic Code in criminal matters.

In modern Israel almost no legislation remains from the Ottoman rule; the Turks did, however, leave their mark on the principles of land law, while their policy of delegating matters of personal status to the various religious communities has continued to this day.

After Turkey's defeat in World War I, Palestine became a League of Nations Mandate 'A' under British administration"[7]. On November 2, 1917, Arthur James Balfour, then British Foreign Secretary, made public a letter known as the Balfour Declaration which stated in part 'His Majesty's Government views with favour the establishment in Palestine of a National Home for the Jewish people ...". The declaration was recognized by the United States in a joint Congressional Resolution.[8]

---

[6] Foundations of Law, 1980; 34 L.S.I. 181

[7] J. Badi. The Government of the State of Israel 10 (1963).

[8] H.J. Res. 322, 67th Cong. (June 30, 1922) 62 Cong. Rec. 9770; 9799-9820 (part 10).

The Palestine Mandate was adopted by the Council of the League of Nations in London on July 24, 1922[9] while United States consent to the administration of Palestine by Great Britain was given on December 3, 1924 in the Convention Between the U.S. and Great Britain, Rights in Palestine, after Turkey had renounced all rights and title over Palestine in favor of the Principal Allied Powers.

At the initiation of the League of Nations' imposed British Mandate, the Palestine Order-in-Council, 1922, declared that "The jurisdiction of the civil courts shall be exercised in conformity with the Ottoman law in force in Palestine 1st November 1911 ... " (the date of the outbreak of hostilities between the Allied Powers and Turkey, of which Palestine at the time was a province). Thus the British Mandate administration, although introducing many legal changes, continued the Ottoman law.

The British rule left an extremely important imprint on the law and government of Israel and was instrumental in introducing common law principles and precedents to the Mandate and later the State. Mandate law comprised basically British legislation in the fields of business and commerce, including the ordinances covering companies, partnerships, banking, bills of exchange and bankruptcy. In other areas there was often a merger of Ottoman laws and English case law.[10]

The Palestine Order in Council, 1922, article 46, sets out the sources of law and determined the supremacy of statute law. It also determined that in cases where there was no relevant statute law - a lacuna - referral was to made to the common law and the doctrines of equity in use in England. In this manner British common law became an important part of Mandate law and continued even after the establishment of the State. This provision was repealed only in 1980.[11]

The continuing clashes and the conflicting interests of the Arab and Jewish communities in Palestine led to the appointment of an Anglo-American Committee of Inquiry. After its report in 1946, the British government proposed a federal scheme - the Provincial Autonomy Plan. As both communities objected to the plan, the entire Palestine question was referred to the United Nations in February 1947. The result was the Partition Resolution of the U.N. General Assembly of November 29, 1947 which proposed the partition of Palestine into two independent states. Upon termination of the Mandate on May 14, 1948 the Declaration of the State of Israel (1 Off. Gaz. (May 14, 1948); 1 L.S.I.3) was issued by the Provisional Government.

---

[9] British Mandate for Palestine, 8 League of Nations Off. J. Annex 391, at 1007 (1922).

[10] For a survey on this subject see Shachar, Y. "History and sources of Israeli law" in Introduction to the law of Israel, ed. A. Shapira (Kluwer, 1995)

[11] Foundations of Law, 1980; 34 L.S.I 181

Almost immediately after the establishment of the State, the Provisional Council enacted the Law and Administration Ordinance which declared that "The law which existed in Palestine on the 5th of Iyar 5708 (14th May 1948) shall remain in force insofar as there is nothing therein repugnant to this ordinance or to other laws ... of the State..." (Off. Gaz. Supp.1 (May 21, 1948); 1 L.S.I. 7). The body of law in force on that date comprised Mandate and Ottoman law. Thus we see continuity from one legal administration to the next.

CHAPTER 2: PRIMARY SOURCES : LEGISLATION AND ISRAEL STATE RECORDS

A. CONSTITUTION

Israel has no formal, written constitution; rather, it was decided - pursuant to the Harari Resolution, 1951 - that separate basic laws, Hukei Yesod, shall be enacted that together will constitute a constitution. To date, eleven such laws have been passed. They are: the Knesset (1958), Israel Lands (1960), President of the State (1964), the Government (1968), the State Economy (1975), the Defense Forces (1976), Jerusalem Capital of Israel (1980), the Judiciary (1984), the State Comptroller, Human Dignity and Freedom, 1992, Freedom of Occupation, 1994.[12] These laws are published in the series of statutes, Sefer HaHukim, which will be discussed below. All official publications are in Hebrew unless otherwise noted.

In addition, many basic principles of human and civil rights are to be found in the Declaration of the Establishment of the State of Israel.[13] The Supreme Court has found a base for some of its human rights decisions in these principles. (For full text of Declaration see appendix)

B. LEGISLATION

According to the Interpretation Ordinance (New Version) 1967,[14] "hok" refers to a legislative act of the Knesset. The translation into English of "hok" is a law or an act. Enactments before the establishment of the state as well as those enacted in the early period (May 19, 1948 - February 10, 1949) are called ordinances. The Law and Administration Ordinance, 5708-1948 was enacted by the Provisional Council and deals with the basics of setting up the new government covering administration of the Provisional Government, budget and taxes, establishment of the Provisional Council of State as the legislative authority, law courts, armed forces and enabled the existing law to remain in force as well as other transitional provisions. The Transition Law, 5709-1949[15] was the first enactment of the first Knesset which took over from the Provisional Council and gave authority to the basic government institutions – the Knesset, President of the State, the Government.

---

[12] For more on the subject see "Basic laws and ordinary legislation." Livneh, Ernst. Israel Law Review 13:251-257, 1978."On the written constitution." Shamgar, Meir. Israel Law Review 9:467-476, 1974 "The new basic laws on human rights: a mini-revolution in Israeli constitutional law?" Kretzmer, David. Israel Law Review 26:238-249, 1992

[13] 1 L.S.I 3, 1948

[14] 1 Dinei Yisrael (Nusah Hadash) 2 (1954); 1 L.S.I. (N.V.) 5.

[15] 3 L.S.I. 3, 1949

The **Rules of the Knesset (Takkanon)** regulate the legislative procedure and call for a first "reading" of a draft law, referral to the appropriate committee, then another two readings. Acts are passed at the third reading, by a simple majority vote of those present and are signed by the Prime Minister, the appropriate cabinet minister and the President of the State. [16] They take effect on the day of publication in the official gazette, Reshumot (see following), unless otherwise stated in the law.[17]

C. RESHUMOT – ISRAEL STATE RECORDS

This is the official gazette of laws, regulations, notices, etc. and may be viewed as a continuation of the series from the Mandate period entitled the Palestine Gazette (Iton Rishmi). Almost all parts of the series retained the previous format and title for the year 1948. Subsequently the size was scaled down and new Hebrew titles instituted for existing sections while several new sections were added.

ACTS AND DRAFT LAWS

1. SEFER HAHUKIM

The collection of laws entitled Sefer HaHukim commenced publication with number 1, February 17, 1949. The numbering then continued consecutively through the years with the acts of November 1999 reaching number 1718. The acts are printed as slip laws and bound at year's end with indices provided by the government printer.

Two volumes of acts precede the current series and include legislation of the newly established state. They continued the title and form of the Mandate Official Gazette (Iton Rishmi) Supplement A. (For more information on this series see the chapter on pre-state materials). These two volumes were published by authority of the Provisional Council, the predecessor to the Knesset. They are: **Iton Rishmi**, **Supplement A,** 1948/49 No. 1, May 19, 1948 - no. 36, Sept. 30, 1948. **Iton Rishmi, Supplement A,** 1949. No. 1, Oct. 14, 1948 - no. 61, Feb. 16, 1949.

2. NUSACH MESHULAV - Consolidated version

In a few instances a number of separate but related laws and amendments were consolidated and re-enacted into law; they were given the subtitle, consolidated version. An example is the Courts Law (Consolidated Version), 1984. These quasi-codes have no special status and are to be found in the general legislative series, Sefer HaHukim. The

[16] A. Rubinstein, Hamishpat Hakonstituzioni (2d Ed. 1974) (Hebrew).

[17] Law and Administration Ordinance, 1 L.S.I. 7, 1948

authorization for this is to be found in sec. 16 of the Law and Administration Ordinance, 1948.

Just a note as to the dates. The State of Israel uses both the Hebrew and Gregorian calendars. The date May 14, 1948, Israel's Independence Day, corresponds to 5 Iyar 5708. The Hebrew year generally begins some time in September of the secular year and runs for twelve months (thirteen in leap years) straddling two secular years. Thus if the Hebrew year is mentioned with no month cited, some confusion may arise as to which secular year the Hebrew year corresponds.

3. HATZA'OT HOK - DRAFT LAWS

"A bill is deemed to be laid before the Knesset when it is handed to the Speaker who tables it and then puts it on the Order of the Day. A Government bill passes three readings."[18]

The draft laws are printed on blue paper, a vestige from the Mandate administration, based on the custom in England. As with most Israel official publications, the sheets or pamphlets can be bound at year's end with title page, index and binding case available from the government printer. The bills are sometimes bound together with the acts, Sefer HaHukim, although it may be considered preferable to keep them separate. The bills are numbered consecutively year after year with number one dated March 11, 1949 whereas 1999 bills have reached number 2,800.

4. DINEI MEDINAT YISRAEL (NUSAH HADASH) - LEGISLATIVE ACTS - NEW VERSION

This series of legislation consists of selected laws originating in the Ottoman or Mandate administrations which are officially translated into Hebrew and re-enacted into law. Thus, the Hebrew version becomes the authoritative one. Even today a portion of Israel statutory law is to be found in the original pre-State enactments by virtue of the Law and Administration Ordinance, 1948, which continued the validity of pre-state legislation.

Number one in the series, the Interpretation Ordinance, is dated January 1, 1954. (Number one carried the series title, Dinei Yisrael; the current title started with number two.) The last act in this series is number 37 enacted in 1983. The series ceased publication, apparently due to the paucity of laws needing to be translated and re-enacted. From 1984/5 such laws appear in the general legislative series, Sefer Hahukim.

[18] Ibid

5. HATZA'OT DINEI MEDINAT YISRAEL (NUSAH HADASH) – DRAFT LAWS OF THE STATE OF ISRAEL (NEW VERSION)

These draft laws are printed on pink paper to differentiate them from the Hatza'ot Hok which were printed on blue paper. No. 1 is dated January 7, 1953 and is entitled Hukei Eretz Yisrael; nos. 2-5 are entitled Dinei Yisrael. The current title commenced with no. 6. The last draft law in this series was in November 1985, number 48, Public Health law. The series ceased publication and any later drafts, if published, will be found in the general series of legislative drafts, Hatza'ot Hok.

D. UNOFFICIAL COMPILATIONS

There exist no official codes or compilations of the law (other than the consolidated version discussed above). However, two private publishers have brought out comprehensive multi-volume compilations of the law arranged alphabetically by the name of the act. (In some cases acts are filed by broad subjects such as education and criminal law.) Both sets are in Hebrew and are supplemented regularly, 3-4 times per year with loose-leaf replacement pages. They reflect the law in force by adding relevant amendments and deleting repealed sections from the text of the original act. In the margin, along side such changes, appear the date and citation of the change. Often regulations in pursuant of the law are included, appearing after the legislative text. For repealed acts reference must be made to the original law as published in Sefer HaHukim (or to the superseded pages if they are kept, which usually is not done). These series - either one or both - are basic tools in legal research and are to be found in virtually every law library.

1. **Hukei Medinat Yisrael**. [Laws of the State of Israel] (3d ed.Tel-Aviv, 35v. loose-leaf)

The original series was published by Robert Gideon. It first appeared in 1953 in bound volumes. The third edition, in loose-leaf format, started in 1984 and is regularly updated (3- 4 times a year) with additional volumes added as necessary. One volume is devoted entirely to a general index. All other volumes contain tables of contents but no indexes.

2. **Dinim.** [Laws] . (Hod Hasharon, 33v. loose-leaf.)

In 1968 Eliahu Winograd, today a retired District Court judge, published this parallel series. It is very similar in format to the above mentioned work having an alphabetical arrangement of legislative acts

which include amendments and repeals. One volume is a general index. It is supplemented 3 - 4 times per year.

2. **Hahakika be'medinat_Yisrael** [Legislation in the State of Israel] edited by Z.H. Preisler. (Jerusalem, Ketuvim, 5 v. loose-leaf).

This is another unofficial compilation of statutes. This set, however, is arranged in broad subject categories which makes searching easier when trying to locate legislation by subject, but a bit more complex when searching for an act by name . Fortunately, it includes alphabetical indexes. This five volume set manages to include all the legislation for which its competitors need over thirty volumes, but it is printed quite densely and in a larger than usual format - folio size. Supplemented 3-4 time per annum.

For statutes in electronic format see the chapter on CD-Roms.

E. TRANSLATIONS

1. OFFICIAL TRANSLATION

LAWS OF THE STATE OF ISRAEL

The Ministry of Justice publishes this authorized English translation of the laws. Forty-two pamphlets have appeared, each covering one Hebrew year, from 1948-1987/8. One unnumbered volume appeared in 1978 entitled, Special volume - Penal Law, 5737-1977. There is a considerable time gap in their publication. Three pamphlets of the New Version have also appeared. Each pamphlet has an index and various tables.

2. UNOFFICIAL TRANSLATIONS

1 - A commercial outfit , **A.G. Publications**, located in Haifa publishes unofficial but reliable translations of many laws and updates them with new revised editions from time to time. They include Israel's "written constitution" – the basic laws, corporate organization, transactions, property law, taxes, economic incentives, social policy and labor law, securities, public utilities and town planning, criminal law, and other laws covering civil wrongs, computers, freedom of information, and insurance. (A.G.Publications, P.O.Box 7422, Haifa 31070; fax:972-4-826-1182)
They have published a number of compilations of laws including:
Commercial Wrongs Law, 1999. New law which supplements provisions in Civil Wrongs Ordinance

Companies Law, 1999. New, long awaited Companies law. Replacement of old law dating back to Mandate administration, although considerable portions of the old ordinance will be retained.
Entry, residence and citizenship - updated, Sept. 1996.
Freedom of Information Law - and relevant regulations and orders. 2d ed, 1999.
International legal cooperation - full text , consolidated and updated translations of Foreign Judgments Enforcement Law , 1958 and International Legal Assistance Law, 1998.
Israel's property laws - completely updated 2d edition including all amendments legislated until September 15, 1991. 1 v. looseleaf.
Israel's real estate and moveable property laws - completely revised and updated verbatim English translations, incorporating all amendments legislated until June 15,1998.
Israel's written Constitution - translations of the Declaration of Independence and of the Basic laws, consolidated and updated as of January 10, 1999. 3d ed. 1999. 1v. looseleaf.
Israel's labor laws - 4th ed. 1999.
Penal law - incorporating all amendments including no.40. 3d ed. 1999.
Preparing for Bug Y2K - compilations of various laws dealing with this topic including securities regulations, rules for reporting on programs to solve problem, investment counseling rules for reporting to customers.
Securities legislation , 1998 - updated and consolidated translations of the Securities Law , 1968 and of relevant subsidiary legislation. 4th ed. 1999. 1v. looseleaf.
Transactions - twenty Israel laws on business transactions and relationships, in up-dated consolidated English translations. 2d ed. 1994- . 1 v. looseleaf.

2 - The Ministry of Labour and Social Affairs publishes every few years new editions of the **Labour Laws**, the latest being from 1994 in 312 pages. This pamphlet includes a wide range of labor related legislation covering twenty-two acts, e.g. Collective Agreements Law, Employment Service, Hours of Work and Rest Law, etc.

3 - The Union for Environmental Defense, **Adam Teva V'Din,** in conjunction with the Ministry of the Environment published in 1993 a pamphlet containing translations of a number of environmental laws entitled Israel's Environmental Legislation and edited by S. Warchaizer. The work is divided into 6 sections covering general provisions, air and noise pollution, fresh water quality, marine pollution, hazardous substances and solid waste, and the protection of nature.

4 - **Business Laws of Israel**, edited and translated by L. Garb, H. Glazer and A. Rachlin, is a one volume looseleaf published in 1997 by Kluwer Law International. It contains translations of laws in the following categories: legal entities, commercial law, banking and financial services, labour law, contract, intellectual property, dispute settlement, fiscal, and bankruptcy.

F. INDEXES

There is a cumulative index to legislative acts called **Mafteah Hapkudot v'haHukim** published by the Ministry of Justice every few years. The latest edition covering just about fifty years, 1948-1997, appeared in 1998 and is entitled Hatehika shel Medinat Yisrael. It comprises an alphabetical list of all the acts in Hebrew with a listing of all amendments, changes and repeals made through the years.

G. CITATIONS

The standard citation to a statute includes the full name of the act, Hebrew year, secular year, name of statute series and page number; for example, Labour Courts Law, 5729-1969, Sefer HaHukim (5729) 70. Rules for uniform citation in Hebrew can be found in the Report of the Committee of Legal Citations, 3d ed, published in 38 HaPraklit 240-258 ,1990; a short supplement appeared in 44 HaPraklit 401- 404, 1998.

A note about the basic laws cited here. Although regular legislation uses the year enacted as part of the name of the law, basic laws are in a special category of entrenched legislation and therefore don't include the year in the citation. In addition, it should be noted that use of the authorized English translation, Laws of the State of Israel (L.S.I.), can be misleading as this series publishes the translation of the original act but does not up-date it with amendments, etc. Thus, we give the citation to L.S.I because it is in English but the reader must be aware that there may be later amendments. The best way to find the law in force including all subsequent changes is by using one of the looseleaf sets of compiled legislation, **Dinim** or **Hukei Medinat Yisrael** (see above) or one of the CD-Roms (see chapter on CD-Roms).

H. PATHFINDER

HOW TO FIND A CURRENT STATUTE

Hebrew

1. Use one of the compilation series edited by **Gideon, Winograd or Preizler** (see above for details) which give alphabetical and subject access to laws in force. They are supplemented several times a year.
2. Alternatively, use may be made of the CD-Roms : **Pad-Or, Takdin, Dinim** , **Gideon 2000,** (see chapter on CD-Roms for details). These are usually updated quarterly.
3. For new legislation which has not been included in these series reference must be made to the slip laws of **Sefer HaHukkim**.

English

1. **Laws of the State of Israel**, as the authorized translation, is usually the first place to start one's search. (see above for details). Be aware, however, that these translations do not include any later amendments or changes. This series, unfortunately, is not kept current; the last issue appeared in 1986/87.
2. There are a number of compilations of unofficial translations of laws usually by subject, such as the publications of **A.G. Publications** and business laws by Garb (see above under Translations).
3. Translations of some laws can be found in **books** dealing with various legal subjects in Israel, e.g. Israeli business law, Public law in Israel, European legal traditions and Israel. (For others see also the Appendix :Bibliography).
4. A. Reference can also be made to **compilations of world laws** on certain topics, e.g. tax, commercial law, copyright.

   B. A detailed bibliography of Israel laws can be found in **Foreign Law: Current Sources of Codes and Basic Legislation in Jurisdictions of the World**, edited by T. Reynolds.

   C. Martindale-Hubbell publishes a volume entitled **International Law Digest** as part of its law directory. Its Israel Law Digest has 16 pages of summaries of the legal status of a wide range of topics including business organizations, regulation and commerce, citizenship, civil actions and procedure, criminal law, debtor and creditor, dispute resolution, employment, environment, estates and trusts, family, intellectual property, property and taxation.
5. Israel **websites** such as those for the Knesset and the Foreign Ministry also have some translations of basic laws and other documents (see chapter on Websites).

CHAPTER 3 : SUBSIDIARY LEGISLATION

Reshumot, Israel State Records, also includes the following sections which will be discussed below. Kovetz HaTakanot, Kovetz HaTakanot: Shiurei Mehes ... , Yalkut HaPirsumim, Hukei Takziv, Yoman HaPatentim v'HaMidgamim, Yoman Simanei Mis'har, Kitvei Amana. All of these series are written in Hebrew while Yoman HaPatentim v'HaMidgamim and Kitvei Amana also include a foreign language.

A. REGULATIONS

1. Kovetz HaTakanot - Collection of regulations or subsidiary legislation. (K.T.)

This is a chronological compilation of the regulations of the various government ministries. Each volume contains alphabetical and subject indexes while a cumulative index appears every few years, the last being 1968. Number 1 of the general series is dated February 25, 1949 and the numbering is continuous through the years. A recent number from September 1998 is #5928. The number is to the pamphlet issued, each one containing several regulations. Title page, index and binding case are available resulting in two large volumes per year.

Until 1957 each volume included indexes to the regulations and the city by-laws. In 1957/58 the index was divided into a general section and local government section. In 1980/81 a separate sub-series of the regulations entitled Local Government Enactments, Hikukei shilton mekomi commenced publication (see below).

2. Kovetz HaTakanot: Shirurei Mehes, Mas Kenia, v'Tashlumei Hova - Subsidiary legislation.

This is a second series of regulations, dealing with customs duties, purchase tax and compulsory payments. It commenced publication on September 22, 1970.

3. Kovetz HaTakanot: Hikukei Shilton Mekomi - Subsidiary legislation - Local Government enactments.

Series commenced in 1980/81 and includes municipal ordinances and by-laws. This date was previously included in the general series Kovetz HaTakanot, see above. It has now reached #604 on February 4, 1999.

B. PUBLIC NOTICES, TREATIES, ETC.

4. Yalkut HaPirsumim - Government notices

Number 1, February 17, 1949 -. Pamphlets are bound into two volumes each year. The notices include registered company announcements, building and planning notices, appointments such as judges and national councils, election results and court notices. Number 4683 appeared in September 1998.

5.Yoman HaPatentim v'HaMidgamim - Patents and Designs Journal

Each pamphlet has both Hebrew and English text. It commenced publication as a separate series in 1968, previously being included in Yoman HaPatentim, HaMidgamim v'Simanei Mis'har - Patents, Designs and Trade Marks Journal - which began, volume 1, in 1948.

6 .Yoman Simanei Mis'har - Trade Marks Journal

Commenced publication as a separate series in 1968, previously being a part of the Patents, Designs and Trade Marks Journal mentioned above.

7. Kitvei Amana - Treaty documents (K.A.)

This series records treaties in one or two foreign languages, usually English or French, and Hebrew. Number 1, February 24, 1949 is the Egyptian-Israeli General Armistice Agreement. In 1999, the treaties reached number 1187. An index for volumes 1 - 16, treaties 1 – 642, appeared in 1968. An index for volumes 17 – 27 appeared in 1985 and covers treaties numbering 643 – 955. A new consolidated index to volumes 1 – 36, covering fifty years of treaties, appeared in December, 1999. A volume of additions and corrections for volumes 1 – 30 appeared in August 1975.

8. Hukei Taktziv - Budgetary laws

This is a series of annual budgets of the government ministries, Number 1 is dated April 7, 1953. There is also a series of draft budgets - Hatza'ot Hukei Taktziv.

9. Dohot Kaspiim - Financial reports

Number 1, June 28, 1953. Ceased publication in 1968.

C. OTHER OFFICIAL PUBLICATIONS

1. Divrei HaKnesset

These are the proceedings of Israel's parliament, the Knesset. Each Knesset sits for four years (generally), each year constituting one session (moshav), while each session includes two assemblies (kenasim) sitting a total of eight months per year.

The set with this name commenced publication on February 14, 1949. However, two volumes preceded it published by the Israel People's Council, May 4 - 14, 1948 and Israel Provisional Council, October 1, 1948 - February 10, 1949.

A listing of the Knessets and corresponding volumes follows.
First Knesset, February 14, 1949 - August 20, 1951, volumes 1-9;
Second Knesset, August 20, 1951 - June 30, 1955, volumes 10-18;
Third Knesset, August 15, 1955 - August 6, 1959, volumes 19-27;
Fourth Knesset, November 30, 1959 - June 24, 1961, volumes 28-31;
Fifth Knesset, September 4, 1961 - June 22, 1965, volumes 32-43;
Sixth Knesset, November 22, 1965 - July 17, 1969, volumes 44-55;
Seventh Knesset, November 17,1969 - Dec. 25, 1973, volumes 56-68;
Eighth Knesset, January 21, 1974 - May 16, 1977, volumes 69-79;
Ninth Knesset, June, 1977 - June, 1981, volumes 80–91;
Tenth Knesset, July, 1981 – July, 1984, volumes 92–99;
Eleventh Knesset, September, 1984 – August 1988, volumes 100–111;
Twelfth Knesset, February, 1989 – March 1992, volumes 112–125
Thirteenth Knesset, July, 1992 – October, 1996
Fourteenth Knesset, November, 1996 - February, 1999
Fifteenth Knesset, July, 1999 -

Separate indexes covering two or three volumes appear regularly.

Divrei HaKnesset are also available via the internet. The Knesset website **www.knesset.gov.il**, has full text from the 11th Knesset to the current.

An English translation of selected debates can be found in a six volume set edited by Netanel Lorch who was the Clerk of the Knesset for many years. The work is entitled **Major Knesset Debates, 1948 –1981.** Originally prepared in Hebrew, it was subsequently translated into English by D. Vanson-Shefer and published by the University Press of America in 1993. It includes debates from the People's Council and Constituent Assembly, 1948 - 49, through the Ninth Knesset, 1981.

2. Takshir

The title is an acronym for **Takanon Sherut Lamedina** - Regulations for government employment. 5th ed, 1972-

Official publication containing administrative orders and instructions concerning terms and conditions of employment in government offices, which are also followed by many public institutions. Multi-volume loose-leaf set which is supplemented 3–4 times per year. Now available on CD-Rom.

3. Kedem

This title is an acronym for **Kovetz Dinei Misim**, collection of tax laws. It is a multi-volume set of loose-leaf volumes containing statutes, regulations and decisions dealing with income tax, property tax, customs duties and tariffs. Ceased publication.

CHAPTER 4 :PRIMARY SOURCES - JUDICIAL DECISIONS

A. COURT ORGANIZATION

Two laws set out the organization and powers of the court system. They are the Basic Law: The Judiciary and the Courts Law (Consolidated Version) - 1984. They establish the principles of authority, independence of judgment and public proceedings. Also set down are the basic rules concerning judges - their appointment, tenure and termination and those of the court system including the right of appeal, retrial and precedent.

The court structure is twofold consisting of the general courts of law (Batei Mishpat) and the specialized tribunals (Batei Din). The general courts include the Magistrates Courts, District Courts and the Supreme Court.

The tribunals exercise a limited jurisdiction both in rem and in personam. They include the Military Tribunals, the Labor Courts and the religious courts, each of which publishes its own series of court reports.

The Courts Law (Consolidated Version) – 1984, unified into one enactment several related laws: the Judges Act, 1953; Court Act, 1957; Small Claims Act, 1976 and the Registrars' Ordinance (New Version), 1971. It came into force on September 1, 1984. Its first chapter deals with the appointment of judges in the courts. There is a mandatory retirement age of 70 years for all judges. The number of Supreme Court judges is determined by the Knesset (legislature) and today is set at 12; there are also temporary appointments. Cases are generally heard by a panel of 3 judges and on some procedural matters by only one judge. Cases requiring a Further Hearing have 5 or more judges sitting in judgment.

B. SUPREME COURT (Bet Mishpat Elyon)

The Supreme Court is the highest court in the land, having jurisdiction as an appellate court from the District Courts in all matters civil and criminal, sitting as a Court of Civil Appeal or as a Court of Criminal Appeal. Sitting as a High Court of Justice (Bet Din Gavoha

laTzedek; abbreviated to Bagatz), it hears causes in the first instance for which no other court offers a remedy. This court is "authorized to issue prerogative writs against state authorities and against other authorities and individuals that operate by virtue of law." [19]

The Supreme Court usually sits with a complement of three justices, however, there is a provision in exceptional cases for a further hearing (diyun nosaf) of five or more justices on a matter which was decided by three. In warranted cases there is a provision for a retrial by the Supreme Court or District Court in a criminal matter.[20] The Knesset, by resolution, determines the number of members of the Supreme Court. It is now set at twelve, previously comprising eleven; however there are sometimes additional temporary appointments.

The doctrine of stare decisis applies in Israel. As Baker states, "Every court will be guided by a rule laid down by a higher court, while a rule laid down by the Supreme Court will bind every court except itself."[21]

REPORTS

1. PISKEI DIN (P.D.)

Judgments of the Supreme Court are published by the court in pamphlets which can be bound at year's end with title page, index and binding cases available. Not every decision is chosen for publication and only about 25% of decisions handed down actually see print. However, the introduction of CD-Roms has made a great impact in this area and they provide the text of cases not published in the official series. See Chapter 7 for information on CD-Roms.

Each decision has headnotes which include a list of pertinent statutes and other sources cited in the decision; there is also a summary of the facts of the case and the ruling – ratio decidendi.

Publishers of the official series have varied through the years. The Ministry of Justice published the set for the years 1948-1970. The Supreme Court itself took over publishing from 1971 to 1978. For the years 1979-1980 a private firm, Microshur, was the publisher; then the Israel Bar Association produced the reports for the years 1981 - 1996. In 1998 the license to print and distribute the reports was awarded to a private firm , Nevo, which started printing with Vol.51 , 1997. It is

---

[19] Shachar,Y. "History and sources of Israeli law" in Introduction to the Law of Israel, ed.A.Shapira. (Kluwer, 1995)

[20] Baker, op. cit. 201.

[21] Baker, op. cit. 202.

trying to bridge the time gap in the delay in publishing and make publication more timely.

There have been a number of changes in the bibliographic details of the volumes published and following is a checklist.

Volume 1, 1948; Volume 2, 1949; and Volume 3, 1949/50 were reprinted in 1956/57. Volume 4 first appeared in 1950, but a second enlarged and corrected edition was published in 1952. Volumes 1 - 4 are composed of one bound volume per year; Volumes 5 - 8 have two bound volumes per year; Volumes 9 - 13 have three bound volumes per year; Volumes 14 - 20 have four bound volumes per year; Volumes 21 - 29 have two bound volumes per year; Volumes 30 - 33 have three volumes per year; Volumes 34 - 44 have four volumes per year; Volume 45, 1991 to the present have 5 volumes per year.

2. PSAKIM ELYON (P.E.)

This was another series of Supreme Court decisions, published unofficially, which appeared during the years 1948-1961, Volumes 1- 52. On the whole, it paralleled the Piskei Din but it did report some cases which do not appear in the official edition.

3. TAKZIR PISKEI DIN

A series of summaries of selected Supreme Court decisions published by a private firm, Hamishpetan. It reports current cases usually within one month of their being handed down. It includes a large number of decisions which never reach publication in the highly select, official reports. Volume 1,1965 - . As of 1998 it also appears in a CD-Rom. (See Chapter 7)

4. SELECTED JUDGMENTS OF THE SUPREME COURT

An authorized translation initiated by the Ministry of Justice and continued by the Supreme Court in conjunction with the Israel Bar Association. Each volume contains a very small number of cases, only a tiny fraction of the cases actually decided by the court. Publication is quite tardy and somewhat sporadic; here is a listing of the volumes that have so far appeared.

Volume 1, 1948 - 53
Volume 2, 1954 - 58
Volume 3, 1958 - 60

Volume 4, 1961 - 62 (published 1975);
Volume 5, 1963 - 65 (1980)
Special Volume, 1962 - 69 (published 1975) containing two leading decisions on the subject of nationality made known in the "Who is a Jew?" debate.
Volume 6 , the General Security Service Pardon Case, 1986 (1988)
Volume 7, 1983 - 1987 (1988)
Volume 8, Constitutional law cases – 1969 - 1988 (1992)
Volume 9, 1977 - 1990 (1995)
Volume 10, 1988 - 1993 (1996)

5. JERUSALEM POST LAW REPORTS

Reported and edited by Asher F. Landau, former President of the District Court of Jerusalem. Jerusalem, Magnes Press, 1993. 247p. Includes summaries ranging from 2-6 pages long of sixty-four Supreme Court cases reported in the Jerusalem Post from 1983 to 1991.

C. DISTRICT COURT (Bet Mishpat Mehozi)

This court has unlimited jurisdiction as a court of first instance in all civil and criminal matters not within the authority of the Magistrates Court and deals with all matters not within the exclusive jurisdiction of any other court or tribunal. It hears appeals from the Magistrates Courts, Municipal Courts and various administrative tribunals. Appeals from the District Court are to the Supreme Court. Cases are heard before a panel of 3 judges or sometimes one judge depending on the gravity of the matter. There are District Courts in the following cities: Jerusalem, Tel-Aviv – Yafo, Haifa, Beer-Sheba, Nazereth.

REPORTS

PSAKIM MEHOZIIM (P.M.)

Decisions of the District Courts of Jerusalem, Tel-Aviv-Yafo, Haifa, Beer-Sheba and Nazareth are included in this series published by the Israel Bar Association. Volume one appeared together with Psakim Elyon. The series numbered volumes 1 - 81 for the years 1948/49 - 1973. The numbering changed in 1973, using only the year citation without a volume number; each year contained three bound volumes. Starting in 1983 selected Magistrates Court opinions were added. The title changed to reflect that fact from 1988/89B to 1990-1. Another

change was made in 1992 , so that the series contains 3 volumes of District Court cases while volume 4 is devoted to Magistrate's Court cases. District Court reports are now also available on CD-Roms - Pador, Takdin. See Chapter 7 for details.

D. MAGISTRATES COURTS (Bet Mishpat Shalom)

The Magistrates Court is a court of first instance and has limited jurisdiction in both civil and criminal matters. It may try offenses which are contraventions or misdemeanors, which are punishable with not more than seven years' imprisonment or payment of a fine. There is no jury system in Israel.

The civil jurisdiction of the Magistrates Courts encompasses actions concerning possession or use of immovable property, whatever the value involved. They may also try other civil actions where the amount involved does not exceed NIS 1 million. An appeal from the Magistrates Court lies to the District Court.

There are Magistrates Courts in the following cities: Jerusalem, Tel Aviv-Yafo, Haifa, Beer-Sheba, Nazereth, Netanya, Bat Yam, Herzlia, Kfar Saba, Petah Tikva, Rehovot, Ashdod, Ashkelon, Hadera, Nahariya, Acre, Bet Shean, Tiberias, and Zefat.

REPORTS

1. PSAKIM SHEL BATEI HAMISPAT HASHALOM

The judicial decisions of the Magistrates Courts have not always been published and, in fact, only starting in 1983 did selected decisions appear in the series of District Court Reports. As of 1992, Magistrates Courts cases constitute volume 4 of each year's District Court reports . See discussion above of District Court reports for more details.

2. Mivhar Piskei Din baMishptei Iriat Tel-Aviv-Yafo

The series of selected decisions of the Tel-Aviv-Yafo municipality is published by the law department of that city and it publishes cases in which the municipality was a party. It includes Magistrates, District and Supreme Court judgments. Volume 1, 1948-59; volume 2, 1959-61; volume 3, 1961-63; volume 4, 1963-66; volume 5, 1966-70; volume 6, 1971-73 (in two volumes).

E. OTHER COURTS

1. LABOR COURTS

Piskei Din la'Avoda

The decisions of the National Labor Court and regional labor courts in Jerusalem, Tel-Aviv, Haifa and Beer-Sheba are published by the Israel Bar Association for the courts. Volume 1, 1954/55 - . Twenty pamphlets per annum.

2. MILITARY COURTS

Piskei Din Nivharim shel Bet Din HaZvai L'irurim

Selected judgments of the Military Court of Appeals: Volume 1, 1948-50 published retrospectively in 1966; 1951 - 53 (1968); 1954 - 55 (1970); from 1956 the volumes appeared with a two or three year time lag. The latest is 1998b.

3. MUNICIPAL, SMALL CLAIMS, FAMILY COURTS

The Courts Law also mandates Municipal Courts dealing with local matters as well as Small Claims Courts which hear cases where the sum of the dispute is not more than NIS 15,000 (as of 1998) – the sum is updated as the need arises. No reports from these courts are published.
The Family Courts were established in 1995 and selected cases appear in the Magistrates Court reports.

4. ADMINISTRATIVE COURT

The Administrative Court Act, 1992 established these courts which hear appeals on administrative decisions by the government minister or other administrative authority. Decisions of the District Courts sitting as Administrative Courts are reported in this series, whose short name is Pada"M. **Piskei Din ... le-Inyanim Minhaliim,** Vol.1,1996/97 - .

F. OTHER REPORTS OF DECISIONS

1. **Kovetz Piskei Din Ezrahiim**

Published by the Income Tax Authority, this series covers income tax, property tax and land appreciation tax cases which were decided in the District and Supreme Courts. Twenty-four issues appear each year. Title page and index are available. Volume 1, 1968 - .

2. **Piskei S'hirut**

These decisions dealing with rent, cooperative housing and property tax are published by Baal Habayit v'Hadayar. This series includes both District and Supreme Court judgments appealed from the Tenancy Tribunal but appears somewhat irregularly. Volume 1, 1954-.

3. **Piskei Din shel Bet Din LeMishma'at Ovdei HaMedina**

Decisions of the government employees disciplinary tribunal are published by the Civil Service Commission (Nitzivut Sherut HaMedina) and appear irregularly. Number 1, 1957-.

4. **Padam**

Decisions of the Israel Bar Association's disciplinary tribunal. Volume 1, number 1, September 25, 1975-.

5. **Piskei Din shel ha-Mosad le-Vituah Leumi**

Decisions of the National Insurance Institute commenced publication Volume 1, 1954/56 and reached Volume 10, 1966/68 when it ceased to appear.

G. RELIGIOUS COURTS AND REPORTS

The Religious Courts Act, 1965 enumerates the religious courts as Rabbinical (Jewish) Courts, Sharia (Moslem) Courts, Christian Courts and Druze Courts. The Rabbinical courts are known as Batei Din Rabbaniim. They deal with cases involving matters of personal status, e.g., marriage, divorce, annulment, alimony, adoption and sometimes inheritance. In addition to the Supreme Rabbinical Court in Jerusalem, there are district Rabbinical Courts in Jerusalem, Tel-Aviv, Haifa, Beer-Sheba, Petach Tikva, Netanya, Tiberias-Zefat, Ashdod, and Ashkelon This division of jurisdiction is a vestige of the Ottoman administration's policy of leaving such matters to the jurisdiction of the particular religious community, which adjudicated in accordance with their own religious laws and customs. This policy continued during the Mandate and into the state.

1. **Piskei Din ha-Rabbaniim**

This is a series of judgments of the Rabbinical courts, which consider matters of personal status and adjudicate in accordance with Jewish law. Published by the Chief Rabbinate with the participation of the Ministry of

Religions, it includes decisions of the district rabbinical courts and the Supreme Rabbinical Court in Jerusalem. Publication has been rather erratic, although of late it has improved. Edited by Rabbis A. Azur, H.S. Rosental, M. Chiger. Published by Gideon Publishers.
Volume 1 appeared in 1953 and Volume 19 was published in 1999.
A cumulative index to volumes one through fifteen appeared in 1994.

2. **Osef Piskei Din**

A volume of decisions of the Supreme Rabbinical Court appeared in 1950, entitled Osef Piskei Din ... (Collection of Judgments of the Supreme Rabbinical Court), edited by Z. Warhaftig. It was published by the Ministry of Justice, Institute for Research Jewish Law.

3. **Psikat Batei ha-Din ha-Rabbaniim ve-hahukim,** 1976.

Edited by the late Rabbi Dov Katz, director of the Rabbinical Courts. This is a collection of abstracts of court decisions arranged by subject dealing mainly with matters of personal status but including some other matters - e.g. labor disputes.

4. **Piskei Din me-Bet ha-Din le-Dinei Mammonot u-leverur yahadut** (**Reports of the Rabbinate Tribunal)**

Deals with both religious and civil law matters decided according to Jewish law. This set is edited by Rabbi Abraham Levin, Chief Judge and was first published in 1993. Volume 1 has two narrow bound volumes one dealing with religious matters the other with the civil cases. Later volumes include both parts in one volume. Volume 5 was published in 1998.

5. **Piskei Din shel Bet Din Azori - Reports of the District Court for Civil Jewish Law - Kiryat Arba-Har Hevron**

This court hears cases between litigants who prefer the application of Jewish Law principles. Edited by Rabbi Yoezer Ariel. Volume 1, 1995.

6. **Leket piskei din be'inyanei dat, v.1-4, [1990?]**
Collection of decisions in religious matters

This is a collection of decisions of the Supreme Court of Israel dealing with religious matters. It was published by the Board of Religious Councils in Israel.

H. INDEXES, DIGESTS and CITATORS

With the advent of CD-Roms containing court decisions and the subsequent ease of searching, the case digests have ceased to appear.

Mafteach Inyanim Meugad

Subject index/digest to Supreme Court decisions, published by Israel Bar Association. Coverage of volumes 1 - 26 of the decisions was published in two index volumes, 1993; index to volumes 27 - 38 was published in one volume, 1986. Volumes arranged alphabetically by subject and include short summary of each case based on the headnotes that appeared in the original decision.

HaPsika

This is an index to reported decisions of the District Courts and the Supreme Court. It was published in the 1960's and 1970's and edited by the late Ze'ev Zeltner, President of the Tel-Aviv District Court. It provided a subject approach to the reports as well as tables of cases and numerical listings by case docket numbers. This multi-volume loose-leaf set was arranged in a complicated manner. Ceased publication.

Mafteah Mihlol HaPsika
Consolidated index-digest of the Israeli common law.

Edited by Dan Bar-Haim and published by Idet Lapraklit. Includes 11 volumes and three volumes of supplements. Provided detailed subject approach to case law and legal periodical literature. Lack of uniformity of subject headings makes use difficult. Ceased publication.

Mafteah Hapsika

Index to case law, edited by A. Fulman. Tel-Aviv: Amishar, 1983. 4v. loose-leaf. Also known as Mafteah haTechni - technical index. Volume 1 - case citator covering only Supreme Court cases. This work gives citations to cases when only the docket number is known. It also lists later cases which cited the original case.
Volumes 2, 3, 4 - Statute citator. Alphabetical listing of statutes giving cases which cited them. Ceased publication.

Mafteah le-piskei din shel Bet HaMishpat Ha-Elyon.

Index to Supreme Court Cases. Edited by H. Cohen. Jerusalem: Ketuvim, 1984 - , loose-leaf.

Statute citator covering Jewish law sources, Ottoman legislation, Israeli legislation, subsidiary legislation, treaties, administered territories legislation. Alphabetical listing of statutes listing cases that cited each statute. Published also is a bound volume covering 1948 - 1983.

I. PATHFINDER

HOW TO FIND A CASE

Hebrew

1. Today the easiest way to find a case by subject, name or docket number is by searching the CD-Roms : **Pad-Or, Takdin, Dinim** (for details see Chapter 7). The CD-Roms have the advantage of including both published and non-published decisions. They generally have coverage of cases from 1980 onward.
2. Cases before the 1980's must be found in the bound volumes of the Supreme Court reports and the District Court reports which started publication in 1948. The print version of these reports has , as of this writing, a lag of 18 months.
3. Newer decisions can be found on websites of the courts as well as the commercial sites of Nevo and Takdin (for details see Chapter 8).

English

1. The series **Selected Judgments of the Supreme Court** is usually the first place to search for English translations; however, it is, unfortunately, woefully inadequate as it publishes a very small number of cases and has a severe time lag. (see above for details)
2. Some periodicals publish digests and summaries of cases, see especially, **Israel Law Review and Israel Yearbook on Human Rights.**
3. A very few cases are summarized in English in the website of the Foreign Ministry.

CHAPTER 5 : PERIODICALS AND COLLECTIONS OF ESSAYS

A. PERIODICALS

Given here is a list of major legal and law-related periodicals in Hebrew and English, published in Israel, in which appear articles of interest to the lawyer and the legal researcher.

1.HEBREW

Alei Mishpat
The law review of the Ramat Gan College of Law. Volume 1, no.1, November, 1999-

Assia
Articles on medicine and Jewish law published by Schlesinger Institute, Shaarei Zedek Hospital, 1968 -

Avaryanut u-Stiya Hevratit - Crime and social deviance
Periodical published by Bar Ilan University, Department of Criminology, Volume 1 - 18, 1973 - 1991

Baduk
Monthly bulletin on consumer affairs. Tel-Aviv, Israel Council for Consumer Affairs, 1998 -

Bezelem
A quarterly journal covering human rights matters in the administered territories. Jerusalem, Israel Information Center for Human Rights in the Territories, 1998 -

Biosphera
Monthly publication of the Office for Environmental Quality. Volume 1, 1972-. Latest issue is Volume 25, no. 3, 1996

Bituach
Israel Insurance Quarterly, 1967 –. Frequency varies. Published by College of Insurance; latest issue 103, June 1999

Et ve-Etika
Summaries of cases heard by the Ethics Committee of the Tel Aviv District of the Israel Bar Association, Volume 1, 1990 -

Globes
Daily newspaper for the business community. Tel-Aviv, Monitin, 1985 - Also available on the web, www.globes.co.il

HaGlima
Bulletin of the Tel-Aviv District of the Israel Bar Association, 1995 -

HaLishka
Bulletin of the Jerusalem District of the Israel Bar Association, 1995 -

HaMador ha-Mishpati
Legal issues concerning insurance agents, published by the Insurance Agents Association, 1994 -

HaMishpat
Law review of the College of Management (Mihlala le-minhal), Law School, 1992 - . Irregular. Issues appear as a special section of the newspaper, HaAretz. Most are later reprinted in bound volumes, v.1 - 4, 1992-1998

HaPraklit
Published by the Israel Bar Association, this periodical commenced publication five years before the establishment of the State, in 1943. It is a widely read legal periodical and publishes articles of a scholarly nature as well as subjects of interest to the legal profession. It appears in Hebrew with brief summaries in English. Volume 1, 1943 - . Four issues per volume. Added title page in English.

HaRashut ha-Shofetet
Bulletin of the court system which publishes notices and news. Volume 19,1993 - . Continues Alon Maarehet Hamishpat, no.1, 1984.

HaSanigor
Articles on issues related to the State Attorney and summaries of criminal cases. Kfar Shmaryahu, Skirot Mikzoiyot, 1997 -

Idkunei Missim
Updates on legislation, regulations and cases on taxation, in addition to articles by M. Cohen, Institute for Tax Consultation, 1983 - .

Iyunei Mishpat
Tel-Aviv University law review. Scholarly articles edited by the law students. Three issues per volume. Volume 1, 1971 -. Added title page in English

Iyunim be-Bikoret ha-Medina
Periodical of the personnel of the State Comptroller's Office, 1960 - .

Kirjath Sepher
Bibliographical quarterly of the Jewish National and University Library. Jerusalem, Magnes Press. Volume 1, 1924/25 - . Comprehensive list of books received at that library, including legal materials.

Kriminologia, Mishpat Plili u-Mishtara
Criminology, Criminal Law and Police Science
Published by Tel-Aviv University, Faculty of Law in cooperation with Israel Police. Volume 1, 1973 -

Mehkarei Mishpat
Bar-Ilan Law Studies. Law review of Bar-Ilan University, Faculty of Law. Volume 1, 1980-. (irregular). Publishes articles by law professors, judges and leading jurists, edited by student staff. Added title page and contents in English.

Mishpat u-Memshal – Law and Government
Law review of Haifa University, Faculty of Law, 1992 –

Mishpat u-Sviva – Law and the Environment
Newsletter of the environmental society, Adam Teva vaDin, 1994 -

Mishpat ve-Tzava – Law and the Army
Articles on military law. Tel-Aviv, Israel Defense Forces. Previously an internal journal but from Volume 8, 1988, also distributed to the public

Mishpatim
Law review of Hebrew University, Law Faculty. Scholarly articles edited by the law students. Three issues per volume. Volume 1, 1968 - . Added title page in English

Missim
Bi-monthly journal of taxation articles. Tel-Aviv, Ronen, 1987 -

Odcan
Current information bulletin for the lawyer. Israel Bar Association and Skira Mishpatit, 1988 -

Plilim
Criminal law periodical. Tel-Aviv University, Faculty of Law, Institute for Criminology, 1990 -

Refuah u-Mishpat - Medicine and Law
Bulletin of the Israel Society for Medicine and Law, 1986 -

Riv'on HaYisraeli leMisim
Quarterly Tax Journal published by the Museum of Taxes and the State Revenue Administration. Volume 1, 1965 -

Rivon leBankaut
Banking quarterly, includes some law related articles. Tel-Aviv, Israel Bank Association, 1961 -

Rivon leCalcala
Economics quarterly, includes some law related articles. Tel-Aviv, 1953 -

Roeh HaHeshbon
The Journal of the Institute of Certified Public Accountants in Israel. Volume 1, 1951 -

Sefer haShana shel ha-Mishpat be-Yisrael
Annual review of the law in Israel. Edited by Prof. A. Rosen-Zvi.Tel-Aviv University, Faculty of Law, and Israel Bar Association, Volume 1, 1991, Volume2, 1992/93, Volume 3, 1996/97

Sha'arei Mishpat
Law review of the Sha'arei Mishpat Law College, Hod HaSharon, Volume 1, 1997 -

Shnaton Mishpat haAvoda
Labor law annual includes academic articles on employment, labor relations, and collective labor agreements. Tel-Aviv, Sadan, 1989 -

Skira Mishpatit
Bulletin of summaries of recent court decisions. Kfar Shmaryahu,1986 - . Frequency irregular, appears about once a month. Also has a fax edition of most recent cases.

Tarbut Demokratit – Democratic Culture
Ed. By A. Sagi and Y. Stern. Studies and essays on the relationship between democracy and Judaism and Zionism. Volume 1, 1999. Ramat Gan, Bar-Ilan University.

Yeda le-Mayda
Monthly publication of articles on taxation, law and economics. Tel-Aviv, Rayonot, 1990 -

Zehuyot haEzrah
Bulletin of the Israel Association for Human Rights, 1981 -

These two periodicals have ceased publication:

Hed HaMishpat. Ed. by J. Harish. Volume 1, no.1, September 26, 1956-no.19/20, July 1958.
Bi-weekly periodical of legal and social problems.

Hok u'Mishpat. Ed. by E. Salant. Tel-Aviv, Hukim Halaha l'Ma'ase. No. 1, December 9, 1954 - no. 24, December 29, 1955.
Legal bi-weekly periodical including articles and law reports.

2. ENGLISH

EcoAdvocate
Published by Adam Teva ve-Din, the Israel Union for Environmental Defense, Volume 1, 1991-

International Association of Jewish Lawyers and Jurists. Bulletin/Newsletter
Published by the Association, from 1970. Title changed in 1994 to **Justice.** Includes articles about legal issues in Israel as well as items about Jewish lawyers abroad.

Israel Annual of Public Administration and Public Policy
Edited by the Israel Institute of Public Administration and the World Institute, Jerusalem. Appeared annually since 1960 under the name of Public Administration in Israel and Abroad; 14 volumes published. New title started with Volume 15, 1976. Publication ceased.

Israel Environment Bulletin

Published by the Ministry of the Environment, Vol.1,1974 -. Latest, Volume 22, no.3, Summer 1999.

Israel Law Review

Scholarly review published under the auspices of the Hebrew University, Faculty of Law, Jerusalem, in English. Four issues per volume. Volume 1, 1966 - . Indexed in Index to Foreign Legal Periodicals.

Israel Yearbook on Human Rights

Volume 1, 1971 -. Tel-Aviv University Faculty of Law. Includes articles on human and civil rights in Israel and the administered territories. It also has translations of excerpts of Supreme Court judgments on these subjects. Annual. Volume 28, 1998

Tel Aviv University. Studies in Law

Faculty of Law, Vol. 1, 1975 - . Scholarly articles in English.
Publication irregular. Vol.14, 1999

Theoretical Inquiries in Law

Contains articles of general interdisciplinary interest; not only Israel law is addressed. Cegla Institute for Comparative and Private International Law, Faculty of Law, Tel-Aviv University. Volume 1, no.1, January, 2000.

B.INDEXES

Index to Legal Periodicals in Israel, 1976 - 1996. Edited by Esther M. Snyder and Batia Razinski. Bar Ilan University, Faculty of Law Library, 1997. 920p. Indexes by subject and author articles in Hebrew and English with about 20% of work in English . Covers all the major legal periodicals, collections of essays and law-related journals including Jewish law publications. Selected articles on Israeli law topics printed abroad are also indexed. There are three sections : (1) Hebrew subject section, (2) author index in Hebrew, (3) author index in English. In addition there is an English glossary with Hebrew equivalents and a reference to the page number in main section.

Index to Cases and Statutes Cited in Periodical Literature, 1978 - 1991. Edited by Batia Razinski. Bar- Ilan University, Faculty of Law Library, 1993. Arranged by case names and names of statutes this citator lists periodical articles which cite the court reports and legislation. Indexes the major legal periodicals in Israel.

Mafteah le-Ma'amarim Mishpatiim. Edited by A. Fulman. Index to periodical articles by topic and sub-topic. No dates given.

C. COLLECTIONS OF ESSAYS

There are a fairly large number of collections of essays, jubilee volumes and festschriften which contain important articles for legal research. Most of them have been indexed in the Index to Legal Periodicals in Israel (see above). Many of the titles start with the word "sefer" which in Hebrew means book. Following is a listing of some of the more important ones.

1.HEBREW

Ba'in Ke-ehad - In inner harmony: essays and articles
Festschrift for the late Supreme Court justice, Moshe Silberg. In addition to five commemorative essays, the volume contains the writings of M. Silberg on a wide range of legal topics including Jewish law and excerpts from his judicial decisions. Jerusalem, Magnes, 1981. 430p. This was reprinted in 1998 in a volume entitled **Kitvei Moshe Silberg** which also includes a short work on the Talmud, entitled **Kach darko shel Talmud.**

Gevurot leShimon Agranat - Essays in honor of Shimon Agranat
A collection of essays in honor of a past President of the Supreme Court on his 80th birthday. Articles by leading jurists and academics. Includes a list of decisions written by Agranat as well as a bibliography of his other writings. Edited by A. Barak and others. Jerusalem, 1987.

Masot baMishpat - Legal essays
A collection of essays by veteran law Professor Gad Tedeschi dealing with the topics: contracts, torts, wills, insurance contracts and agency. Jerusalem, Hebrew University, 1978. 393p.

Masot Nosafot baMishpat - Legal essays (2)
An additional volume of essays by G. Tedeschi. Hebrew University, 1992. 201p.

Masot al Hok uMishpat - Essays on Jurisprudence
Essays by Augusto J. Levi, law professor at Hebrew University, on commercial law, agriculture and constitutional law. Includes reprints and translations of articles and lectures. Jerusalem, Magnes, 1969. 207p.

Mehkarei Mishpat le-Zeher Avraham Rosenthal
Festschrift in memory of A. Rosenthal. Fourteen essays on various legal topics. Edited by G. Tedeschi. Hebrew University, Faculty of Law. Jerusalem, Magnes, 1964. 462p.

Mehkarim beMishpat Artzenu
Early studies on law in the newly established state by G. Tedeschi. Jerusalem, Magnes, 1952. 232p.

Mehkarim beMishpatenu haPrati
Studies on private law by G. Tedeschi. Deals with specific topics in contracts, torts, marriage and succession. Jerusalem, Mifal Hashihpul, 1958. 369p.

Minha le-Yitzhak
Jubilee volume in honor of the District Court Judge Yitzhak Shilo. Includes general essays on the law in Israel, Jewish law, civil and commercial law, family law and state and religion, criminal law, international law, and courts and procedure written by leading judges and law academicians. Edited by A. Barak and M. Shawa. Israel Bar Association, 1999.

Mishpat Plili, Kriminologia u-Mishtara - Criminal law, criminology and police science
Articles dealing with these subjects written by law professors and lawyers, edited by G. Orion. Tel Aviv University, 1986.

Mishpat veShiput - Justice and the judiciary: a collection of articles and notes
A volume of writings of the late Supreme Court justice, Alfred Witkon dealing with the judiciary and articles in his field of specialization, taxation. Tel-Aviv, Schocken, 1988.

Sefer Bar-Niv - In memoriam Zvi Bar-Niv
A collection of articles on labor law written by leading jurists in memory of the late President of the National Labor Court. Edited by A. Barak, M. Goldberg and others. Articles in Hebrew, English, French and German. Tel-Aviv, Ramot, 1987. 213,283p.

Sefer Berenson

Jubilee volume in honor of Zvi Berenson, past Supreme Court justice. Edited by A. Barak and H. Berenson. Includes biographical essays, articles on law and ethics, and judicial decisions on such topics as torts, public law, labor law, and procedure. Jerusalem, Nevo, 1997. 408p.

Sefer Itzhak Kahan

Festschrift in memory of the President of the Supreme Court, Itzhak Kahn. Edited by M. Elon and others. Tel-Aviv, Papyrus, 1989. 455p. Includes reports of committees chaired by Justice Kahan including Polygraph Committee, Committee on the protection of privacy, Commission of Inquiry into the events in the refugee camps in Beirut, 1983. Articles deal with the subjects Jewish law, public law, the courts, criminal law, and private law.

Sefer Klinghoffer al haMishpat haZiburi - Klinghoffer Book on Public Law

Commemorative volume for H. Klinghoffer, veteran professor of law at Hebrew University. Includes his own articles and those of other well-known jurists on public law issues. One section deals with the authority of the Attorney-General. Edited by Y. Zamir. Jerusalem, Sacher Institute, 1993. 507p.

Sefer Landau

Jubilee volume in honor of past Supreme Court Justice Moshe Landau. Edited by A. Barak and E. Mazoz. Tel-Aviv, Bursi, 1995. 3v. Volume 1 - Writings - articles and lectures of Justice Landau and reports of public committees which he chaired - Committee on quasi-judicial bodies, Committee on the structure and authority of the courts, Committee on judicial ethics, Committee of Inquiry on methods of inquiry of the General Securities Service in the matter of terrorist activity, as well as his judicial decisions.

Volumes 2, 3 - articles on the courts, public law, criminal law, procedure and contracts, torts and family law.

Sefer Lowenberg

A collection of studies in memory of Judge H.S. Lowenberg. Includes sections on taxation, interpretation, obligations and remedies, business entities and road safety. Edited by D. Friedmann and Y. Shiloh. Tel-Aviv, Bursi, 1989, 293p.

Sefer Sussman
Festschrift in memory of Yoel Sussman, past President of the Supreme Court. Edited by A. Barak and others. Articles dealing with public law, civil law, procedure, criminal law and international law in addition to speeches given at a memorial service. Jerusalem, 1984. 424p.

Sefer Uri Yadin - haish upoalo
Jubilee volume in honor of Uri Yadin, former head of the Legislative Drafting Department of the Ministry of Justice. Includes articles in Hebrew and English. Edited by A. Barak and T. Shepnitz. Tel-Aviv, Bursi, 1990. 2v.

Sefer Yovel le-Pinhas Rosen
Jubilee volume in honor of former Justice Minister. Edited by Haim Cohn. Jerusalem, Mifal Hashihpul, 1962. 284p.

Sefer Zicaron le-Ariel Rosen-Zvi - Rav tarbutiyut bemedina demokratit veyehudit - Multiculturism in a democratic and Jewish state.
Collection of essays on the topic of cultural pluralism in a democratic and Jewish state, dedicated to the memory of Professor Ariel Rosen-Zvi, Dean of the Faculty of Law, Tel-Aviv University. Edited by M. Mautner and others. Tel-Aviv, Ramot, 1998, 755p.

Sefer Zicaron le-Procaccia - Essays on law
Festschrift in memory of Gualtiero Procaccia, long time professor of law at Hebrew University. Edited by A. Barak and others. Includes essays written by Professor Procaccia and other legal academics on the legal profession, legal history, business organizations, civil law. Includes a bibliography of more than 60 of his writings. Jerusalem, Sacher Institute, 1996. 410p.

Sefer Zicaron le-Tedeschi - Masot baMishpat Ezrahi
Essays in memory of Gad Tedeschi, long time professor of law at Hebrew University. A collection of essays on jurisprudence and civil law. Includes a bibliography of more than 100 books and articles. Edited by Y. Englard and others. Jerusalem, Sacher Institute, 1995. 669p.

Sugiyot Nivharot Bamishpat - Selected legal topics
A collection of masters' essays submitted to the law faculty of Hebrew University, 1958. 529p.

2. ENGLISH

Introduction to the Law of Israel
Includes articles on the history and sources of Israeli law, the institutional organization of the Israeli legal system, Constitutional law, Administrative law, Family and inheritance law, Contract law, Tort law, Property law, Commercial law, Corporate law, Labour law, Tax law, Criminal law, Criminal procedure, Civil procedure, Evidence, Insolvency, Arbitration, Private international law, International law and the State of Israel. Articles written by "established experts" from academia. Edited by A.Shapira and K.DeWitt-Arar, Tel-Aviv University, Faculty of Law. Hague, Kluwer, 1995. 424p.

The Law of Israel: General Surveys
Seven surveys of major fields of law: constitutional, administrative, international, criminal, contract, property and torts written by leading law professors. Edited by I. Zamir and S. Colombo. University of Haifa, faculty of law. Jerusalem, Hebrew University, 1995. 520p.

Selected Essays - Haim H. Cohn
Jubilee volume in honor of a past justice and vice-president of the Supreme Court. Presents reprints of articles written by Justice Cohn on the subjects of human rights law, Jewish law, speeches, dissenting opinions. Includes a bibliography of over 200 items. Edited by A. Barak and R. Gabizon. Tel-Aviv, Bursi, 1991.

Studies in Israel Private Law
By G. Tedeschi. Translation of the volume "Mehkarim bamishpatenu haprati", published in 1958. See above.

For more works see also Appendix: Selected bibliography.

CHAPTER 6 : REFERENCE BOOKS

Index to Legal Periodicals in Israel, 1976 - 1996

Edited by E.M. Snyder and B. Razinski, Bar-Ilan University, Faculty of Law Library, 1997. 920p. Indexes by subject headings and authors articles in Hebrew and English with about 20% of work in English . Covers all the major legal periodicals and law-related journals including Jewish law publications published in Israel. Covered also are selected articles printed abroad on Israeli legal/ Jewish law topics. There are three sections : (1) Hebrew subject section, (2) author index in Hebrew, (3) author index in English. In addition there is an English glossary with Hebrew equivalents and reference to page number in main section to facilitate use.

Israel Government Publications - Reshimat Pirsumei Memshala

An annual list of government publications received in the State Archives, arranged by government offices and within each office by divisions, departments, etc. Publications in Hebrew and Arabic are entered in the Hebrew section and publications in Latin script are entered in the English section. Publications of local authorities, state corporations and the Army are entered selectively. There are two indexes - Hebrew and English - with listing by author, title/key words. Compiled by S. Yonai. It is very helpful for reference, cataloging and acquisitions. Volume 91, 1998. Also available in microfiche.

Israel Government Yearbook - Shnaton HaMemshala

Gives details of the various government ministries, their functions and staffs, addresses and phone numbers. Published by the Ministry of Education and Culture, Central Office of Information. Articles in Hebrew with about one third of the information on names and addresses appearing in English. Last volume 1998 ,covers government as existed before last elections on May 17, 1999. Appeared in English version, 1950 - 1973.

Israel Legal Bibliography in European Languages

Compiled by E. Livneh. Covers state and pre-state publications. Hebrew University, 1965. 118p. Continued by **A Bibliography of Israel law in English and other European Languages**. Edited by J.R.Wegner. Jerusalem, Hebrew University, Faculty of Law, Institute for Legislative Research and Comparative Law, Series no. 24, 1972. 124 p. **Supplement** 1972-79. Edited by J.D.Wilkenfeld. **A Bibliography of Israeli law in European languages 1990-1995**. H. Bonk. Jerusalem, Hebrew Univ.

Faculty of Law. Sacher Institute for Legislative Research and Comparative Law, 1998.

Israel 50 years - a History in Documents

Ed. By Y. Liebermann and W.van der Wolf. Includes over 100 documents from the Balfour declaration of 1917, U.N. resolutions, cease-fire agreements, peace treaties, and declarations and letters concerning Israel's relationship with its Arab neighbors. Global Law Assoc., 1998.

Israel Yearbook and Almanac

Basic guide to state matters. Gives yearly chronology of events, in-depth surveys of important events, political documents, general data and statistical information. Ministry of Defense, Volume 53, 1999.

Legal Dictionary, English-Hebrew

Compiled by Eliahu Moses, 1990. 325p.

Legal Dictionary, Hebrew-English

Compiled by Eliahu Moses, 2d ed. 1995. 446p.

Concise dictionary compiled by veteran lawyer, fairly authoritative with very brief definitions.

Legal Dictionary, English-Hebrew, Hebrew-English

Edited by E. Shaked, A. Hacohen. Steimatzky, 1992. 236, 197p. Concise work, somewhat simplistic.

Legal Dictionary, English-Hebrew

Compiled by M. Shely. Jerusalem, Dvir, 1982. 107p. A concise dictionary of legal terms from English to Hebrew. Compiled by a former employee of the Ministry of Justice.

Leksikon Lemunahei ha-Hok ha-Israeli.

Lexicon of Israeli legal terms. Edited by A. Lorch and A. Fulman. Keter,1988. List of legal terms and their definitions as found in legislative acts and regulations. Looseleaf. Not updated.

Madrikh haKnesset vehaMemshala

Guide to the Knesset and the government. Tel-Aviv, Policy, 1999. List of members and biographical information, committees, ministers, etc. of the 15th Knesset.

Mafteah Hapkudot vehaHukim

This is a cumulative index to legislative acts published by the Ministry of Justice every few years. The latest edition, covering just about fifty years, 1948-1997, appeared in 1998 and is entitled Hatehika shel Medinat Yisrael. It has an alphabetical list of all the acts in Hebrew with a listing of all the amendments, changes and repeals made through the years.

Mafteach Inyanim Meugad

Subject index/digest to Supreme Court decisions, published by Israel Bar Association. Coverage of Volumes 1 - 26 of the decisions published in two index volumes, 1993; index to Volumes 27 - 38 published in one volume, 1986. Volumes arranged alphabetically by subject and include short summary of each case based on the headnotes that appeared in the original decision.

Report of the Committee on Standard Rules of Citation , 3d ed.

Authoritative rules for legal citation in Israel including abbreviations. Covers statutes, cases, periodicals and monographs. Includes also Jewish law literary sources. 38 Hapraklit 240 - 258 ,1990;
Supplement, 44 Hapraklit 401 - 404, 1997.

Who's Who in Israel

Listing of well-known personages in Israel and Jewish personalities all over the world. Includes many judges, government ministers, members of Knesset, and prominent lawyers and doctors, as well as those from the business and entertainment fields. Volume 22, 1992/93.
Also published in Hebrew as **Mi Vami be-Israel,** Volume 9, 1996.

STATISTICS:

Court activities - Peulot batei hamishpat

Lists and diagrams of procedures in the various courts. Central Bureau of Statistics, 1995-1997.

Criminal statistics - Statistica plilit

Annual publication which presents data on investigation files, grievous offenses committed, indictments and convictions in the courts, various types of criminal offenses and the time elapsed between the date the crime was committed and the conviction. Also given is information on the characteristics of convicted adult and juvenile offenders, the type and severity of penalties imposed and the rates of delinquency in various population groups. 1951 - . Latest published 1995.

Criminal Statistics in Israel

Edited by O. Schmelz. Two volumes of statistics from 1949 to 1961, published by Hebrew University.

Judicial Statistics - Statistica Mishpatit

Annual published by the Central Bureau of Statistics which presents data on civil and criminal matters entered, decided and pending in various courts. The data include detailed classification of matters by type, mode of commencement, cause of action, hearing of testimony, filing of objection, and mode of disposal. 1951 - . Latest 1994-96.

National Insurance Institute. Annual Survey, 1997/98. Skira Shnatit

Edited by G. Yaniv. Jerusalem, 1998. Includes a review of trends in national insurance system [social security], changes in benefits and scope of population, incidence of poverty and inequality in income distribution. Also includes a review of programs to reduce unemployment and an appendix of publications of research reports and surveys. In Hebrew with an English summary.

Statistical Abstract of Israel

Central Bureau of Statistics. Includes information on population, foreign trade, prices, labor and wages, banking and insurance. Court matters are found under the category of public order and include statistics arranged by subject matter and name of court. Most recent Volume 49, 1998.

CHAPTER 7 : CD-ROMS

There are a number of CD-Roms now available in Israel which provide judicial decisions and statutes. Many are parallel works containing identical or at least very similar coverage. An important component of these materials is the inclusion of decisions that were not published in any other format and thus they have enlarged the base of judicial decisions accessible for legal research. As there are continuing retrospective additions, the dates of inclusion of materials mentioned below are accurate as to the time of writing.

1. PAD-OR

Published by the Israel Bar Association, this was the first CD-Rom to appear in Israel. Includes Supreme Court decisions published since 1981 as well as unpublished ones handed down since 1985. District Court decisions published since 1980 as well as selected District Court and Magistrates Court decisions from 1991 to current. The reports also include a short precis of each case prepared by the editorial staff of the Bar Association which was responsible for publishing the court reports for many years. Also included are Military Appeals Court cases from 1996 to current. Decisions of the Israel Lands Administration also appear here. Legislation, both primary and secondary , is given. Future versions will include the Index to Legal Periodicals in Israel published in book form by Bar Ilan University Faculty of Law Library.

Modes of searching are either by a list of index terms or search of full text with boolean operators, and also includes search by case names, as well as by citation or docket number. Separate searches must be done on published and unpublished decisions databases. Version 16, April 1999. Updated quarterly.

2. PAD-OR - BITUAH veNEZIKIN

This CD is based on the format of the above Pad-or but includes only materials on insurance and torts. It covers Supreme Court and District Court decisions both published and unpublished as well as relevant legislation. Latest update December, 1998.

3. PADA'OR

Comprises decisions of the Labor Courts both those that were published in book form and those that were not published. Included also are decisions of the Supreme Court dealing with matters of labor law; labor law statutes; and the Takshir which contains the rules and

regulations of the Civil Service. Published by the Israel Bar Association. Version 5, February 1999. Updated quarterly.

4. TAKDIN

This CD-Rom brings Supreme Court decisions published since 1972 and those unpublished from 1985, District Court and Magistrates Court reports from 1990, District Labor Court reports from 1990 and decisions of the National Labor Court from 1969 to date. Searching is done with index terms or by full text searches. Primary legislation appears here together with any changes, amendments or repeals integrated into text of the acts. In addition there is an index to general Hebrew periodicals prepared by Haifa University Library which covers some legal journals. Latest version April 1999, updated quarterly. This is kept up to date between versions by an online fee-based service, Takdinet, www.takdinet.net.il.

5. DINIM veOD

This is the CD-Rom version of the published set of legislation entitled Dinim and edited by E. Winograd (for more on this set see Chapter 3). It also includes published Supreme Court decisions from 1970 to date and unpublished decisions from 1985 to date as well as selected District Court reports both published and unpublished. Version 22, May 1999, updated quarterly. It is supplemented by an online service www.halachot.co.il.

6. AVODA veOD

This CD is devoted to labor law materials including cases from the National and District Labor Courts, both published and unpublished; cases from the Supreme Court dealing with labor law ; primary and secondary legislation on labor law ; collective agreements; and the Takshir - the rules and regulations of the Civil Service. It also brings the full text of a leading work entitled Labor Law - Individual and Collective by retired Labor Court Judge N. Gutman. Published by Dinim. Version 7, March 1999.

7. MISSIM veOD

A CD devoted to tax law materials including statutes, cases and articles from the periodical **Missim**; the "Habak" - a systematic commentary on the Income Tax Ordinance; tax treaties; professional circulars (hozrim mikzoiim) and a list of public institutions. Included also is the text of the work Value Added Tax Law byY. Potshebuzki. Version 9, December 1998.

8. SAVIR

This CD is based on the published set of Supreme Court case abstracts, Takzir Piskei Din, and includes abstracts from 1966 to date. It also brings full text of most of the cases from 1985 to date. Latest version 1999.

9. GIDEON 2000

New CD covering legislation only. Search engine problematic.

10. RESPONSA PROJECT

This is an outstanding and comprehensive collection of Judaica materials dating back hundreds of years collected, organized and made digitally accessible by the Bar Ilan University Computer Center. It contains numerous works of Jewish Law and has become an essential research tool. The term responsa refers to the rabbinic literature of questions posed to leading Rabbis and their reasoned answers/decisions . (For more information see Chapter 9 - Jewish Law) . This CD, which originally included only responsa, has since been enlarged to encompass the full text of most of the main works of Jewish law. In addition to the "primary" materials : Bible, Mishna, and the Talmud, it comprises hundreds of commentaries ranging from the classic commentators, e.g. Rashi, Ramban – and others through the ages to modern times. Its full text search engine is very well developed to take into account the numerous variations of words in the Hebrew syntax. It was the first CD and search engine produced in Israel and was a world leader in creating the algorithms of full text searching, first appearing in the early 1970s.

Its contents include:

Bible, commentaries on the Bible, Mishna (Jewish Law code), Tosefta (additions to the Mishna not included in the codification), Babyloniam Talmud, Rashi's commentary on the Talmud and Tosfot, Jerusalem Talmud, Midrashei halacha, Midrashei aggada, Zohar, Rambam, Tur, Bet Yosef, Shulhan Arukh (Code of law) and commentaries, Responsa - first generation through to contemporary times.Version 7, 1999. Produced by Bar Ilan University, Responsa Project, Ramat Gan.

CHAPTER 8 : ISRAELI LEGAL WEBSITES

There are a number of Israeli websites on the internet dealing with legal matters which provide current, up-to-date information. The majority of them are in Hebrew although some do have data in English.

OFFICIAL SITES

KNESSET - **www.knesset.gov.il**

The Knesset, Israel's parliament has an excellent site, attractively designed. It has much information on the organization and structure of the Knesset, a Knesset tour, information on Knesset members and parliamentary groups , a section on the electoral system well as selected important documents including the **Proclamation of Independence, the basic laws and documents relating to the peace process**.

The full text of the **Basic laws** include: President of the State, the Knesset, the Government, the Judiciary, the Israel Defense Forces, Jerusalem - Capital of Israel, Israel Lands, the State Comptroller, the State economy, Human Dignity and Liberty, Freedom of Occupation.

It has links to other government sites and national institutions. The site has both Hebrew and English language interfaces. The proceedings of the Knesset, **Divrei HaKnesset,** are available in full text on this site from the 11th Knesset to date including the current 15th Knesset.

COURTS - **www.court.gov.il**

The courts site is another attractive site with much information on the court system and judges in Hebrew and in English. It has a section on the judicial authority as well as detailed information on the status, powers and composition of the Supreme Court, District Courts, Magistrates Courts and Juvenile Courts. The section on judges covers the appointment, qualifications, term of office and other related data. The Hebrew section contains a full listing of all sitting judges and their courts. The site has **decisions of the Supreme Court and National Labor Court** in Hebrew only. It recently added a translation into English of the case on interrogation methods of General Security Services and may continue to translate current cases of international interest. The search engine, theoretically, allows searching by names of cases ; in practice it doesn't actually work; however, it may be searched by docket number. The site is slated to include decisions of other courts as well at a future date.

FOREIGN MINISTRY - **www.israel-mfa.gov.il** or **www.israel.org**

The Foreign Ministry has built an informative, aesthetic site, in Hebrew and English, covering many frequently asked questions about the structure and government of the State of Israel and "provides basic information about Israel and its people, while offering comprehensive material on the Israeli government and its policies." It's sections include: Facts about Israel, Israel by Timeline, Foreign Affairs , Israel at 50 and beyond, the Government, the Law, Personalities, Peace Process, Culture, Economy , and Religion. The section on the **Peace process** has many documents in English.

The section on Law contains four subsections : **basic laws, the judiciary, selected laws, and legal issues and rulings.**

1 - The subsection on **basic laws** includes full text of those laws, which are also available on a number of other sites including the Knesset.

2 - The subsection on **Selected laws** includes: Declaration of Independence, 1948; The Law of Return, Protection of Holy Places, Nationality law (summary), Prevention of Terrorism Ordinance, 1948; Nazi and Nazi Collaborators (Punishment) Law, 1950; Denial of Holocaust (Prohibition) Law, 1986; Party Financing Law, 1973; Golan Heights Law, 1981; Implementing Gaza-Jericho Agreement, 1994; National Health Law, 1995 (summary), Israel's environmental laws.

3 - The subsection on **Legal issues and rulings** includes various items of possible interest from 1990, such as the Supreme Court judgment on legality of interrogation methods (September, 1999), expulsion orders, conscientious objection, Demjanuk case - facts and legal details, Hebron massacre, Israel's settlements - conformity with international law, etc.

4 - The subsection on the **Judiciary** is excellent and has a survey and explanation of the court system in Israel, as well as a list in English of the current Supreme Court Justices.

The Ministry's Information Office also handles requests for information from the public via the site or email **ask@israel-mfa.gov.il**

ISRAEL GOVERNMENT - **www.info.gov.il**

State of Israel Government Gateway - Sha'ar HaMemshala . Very informative, well designed site in Hebrew and English listing all the government ministries, their functions and personnel, as well as links to other official sites including those mentioned above and the President, Bank of Israel, Central Bureau of Statistics, Standards Institute, Social Insurance Institute, etc. An alternative site **www.israel-info.gov** has similar information in non-graphic format.

MINISTRY OF JUSTICE. **www.justice.gov.il**
Site under construction. Data in Hebrew. Has information on the structure of the office, press releases, a section on databases which includes trademarks and property assessors, and a section on State Records which as of this writing includes Public Notices (Yalkut HaPirsumim) and Regulations (Kovetz HaTakanot).

ENVIRONMENTAL LAWS OF ISRAEL.www1.huji.ac.il/www_teva_law

OTHER OFFICIAL SITES include

The President, **www.knesset.gov.il/president/epres_page.htm**
Prime Minister, **www.pmo.gov.il**
The Antitrust Authority, **www.antitrust.gov.il.**
Israel Lands Administration,**www.mmi.gov.il** ,
Central Bureau of Statistics,**www.cbs.gov.il.**
Government Corporations Authority, **www.gcs.gov.il.**
Bank of Israel, **www.bankisrael.gov.il.**
Government Printing Office, **www.gpo.gov.il.**
Embassy of Israel, Washington, D.C. **www.israelemb.org**

It provides information about the embassy and the Foreign Ministry, documents in English on the peace process and sometimes summaries in English of Supreme Court decisions.

OTHER ISRAELI SITES

ISRAEL BAR ASSOCIATION **www.israel.bar.org.il**

This new site has both Hebrew and English sections. The English section contains profiles and objectives of the Israel Bar association; admission requirements to the bar; a list of courses for foreign lawyers; and a section on the International Association of Jewish Lawyers & Jurists. As of this writing the site is not complete.

CONVENTION ON INTERNATIONAL SALE OF GOODS
www.biu.ac.il/law/cisg
Site which covers the status of the U.N. Convention on International sale of Goods in Israel. Prepared and maintained by Dr.Arie Reich of Bar Ilan University.

BTSELEM - ISRAEL CENTER FOR HUMAN RIGHTS
www.btselem.org
Provides information on human rights matters in Israel and the administered territories. Includes some translations of relevant court cases.

COMMERCIAL SITES

DINIM **www. halachot.co.il**
This site has updates of reports and statutes for the CD of the same name. It gives summaries of latest legal developments including legislation, draft bills, regulations and public announcements. The information is in Hebrew. As of this writing there is no charge.

HAIM RAVIA **www.law.co.il**
Maintained by a private lawyer, this site has lots of information in Hebrew and English, including many links to Israeli sites mentioned above, as well as links abroad for the Israeli lawyer. No charge .

LAWDATA **www.lawdata.co.il**
Private site maintained by a lawyer, Alex Hartman. It has current court decisions, statutes, draft bills and a special section on legal information found in newspapers. Hebrew. No charge.

NEVO **www. nevo.co.il**
This site has recent, current decisions and those dating back to 1997 from the Supreme Court, District Courts, Magistrates Courts, Labor Tribunals and Family Courts. Nevo is the publisher of Supreme Court decisions in paper format as of 1998. Subscription required.

SKIRA MISHPATIT **www.interlaw.co.il**
This is a site based on the publication of the same name which publishes weekly summaries of selected court decisions in civil matters from 1985. The site has full-text of selected important decisions from 1996. In addition it has summaries of criminal cases as they appeared in the periodical, HaSanegor, from 1996.

TAKDINET **www.takdin.net.il**
This site updates its CD by the same name and gives current decisions, statutes, and indexing to legal literature. Hebrew. Subscription required.

WALLA **www.walla.co.il**
This general site also has a section on law with links to many legal websites in Israel including lawatch from Haifa University, lists of lawyers, etc.: www.mishpat.com; legalnet.co.il; mishpat.net.
Worth checking.

LAW FACULTIES IN ISRAEL

There are four university law faculties in Israel each of which has its own homepage and whose electronic catalogs, using the program Aleph, are accessible through the web. This OPAC also has a union list of monographs, ULM, and a union list of serials, ULS. There are also non-university law schools some of which may have home pages.

BAR ILAN UNIVERSITY, FACULTY OF LAW **www.biu.ac.il/law/lawlib**

Catalogs of all libraries accessible via - **www.biu.ac.il/lib/aleph.htm**

HAIFA UNIVERSITY - **www.haifa.ac.il**

HEBREW UNIVERSITY, FACULTY OF LAW **www.atar.mscc.huji.ac.il**

TEL-AVIV UNIVERSITY, FACULTY OF LAW - **www.tau.ac.il**

OTHER SITES

There are a number of sites outside of Israel which provide links to the Israel sites. The foreign primary law sites do not provide original work but all list links to sites which have translations of legislation. It should be pointed out that the only acts translated on the web sites, as of this writing, are the Basic laws which are a few specific pieces of legislation setting out general principles and together form a constitution. These are found on the Knesset site and the Foreign Ministry site.

There is no service that provides translations of current statutes on the web, other than a few, selected acts on the Foreign Ministry site. This being said, here are some of the sites based in the United States which provide links.

CORNELL LAW SCHOOL - LEGAL INFORMATION INSTITUTE
www.law.cornell.edu. Legal materials around the globe.

FOREIGN PRIMARY LAW ON THE WEB
Listing of links by country, prepared by T. Mulligan, O"Quinn Law Library, University of Houston. **www.law.uh.edu**

HOUSE OF REPRESENTATIVES. INTERNET LAW LIBRARY
www.infoctr.edu/ill/
This resource prepared by the U.S. House of Representatives, Law Library has ceased being made available by them but can now be found in a number of other host sites. Among the wealth of information in this database, there is also a country division which includes a section on Israel. It includes the Basic Laws of Israel, some other major laws and selected decisions, documents on the peace process, and some papers prepared by the U.S. State Department.

INTERNET LEGAL RESOURCE GUIDE: ISRAEL
www.ilrg.com/nations/il/
Eclectic site listing information culled from other sites on the web especially those already mentioned above.It does a good job of organizing the topics and their links.

LAW LIBRARY OF CONGRESS - GLIN - Global Legal Information Network. **http://lcweb2.loc.gov.glin/israel.html**

SITES OF GENERAL INTEREST IN ISRAEL

GLOBES - **www.globes.co.il**
Daily newspaper on economic matters, some law. Hebrew and English.

HA'ARETZ - **www3.haaretz.co.il/eng/htmls/1_1.htm**
Daily Hebrew newspaper with English version

ISRAEL EXPORT INSTITUTE - **www.export.gov.il**
Information on Israeli exporting firms, products and cooperative ventures.

ISRAEL ONLINE - **www.iol.co.il**
News, tourism, business and other general information in Hebrew.

ISRAELWIRE - **www.israelwire.com**
Latest news in English

JERUSALEM POST - **www.jpost.com**
Daily newspaper in English, internet edition. Can search archives for articles on recent legislation and court cases.

PALESTINIAN LEGISLATIVE COUNCIL
In construction as of this writing. **www.pal-plc.org**

UNITED STATES INFORMATION SERVICE - ISRAEL
www.usis-israel.org.il
Has lots of information on U.S.-Israel relations including reports of developments, documents, etc. Also includes information about the U.S. Embassy in Israel.

YELLOWPAGES - **www.yellowpages.co.il/yp/yp/cgi**
Search for business or products, Hebrew and English. Can search for lawyers by city in English.

CHAPTER 9 - JEWISH LAW

A. INTRODUCTION

The Foundations of Law act, 1980 was legislated to encourage the use of Jewish legal sources. Section one of this short law follows:

> 1. Where the court, faced with a legal question requiring decision, finds no answer to it in statute law or case law or by analogy, it shall decide it in the light of the principles of freedom, justice, equity and peace of Israel's heritage.[1]

In addition, the **Basic Law: Human Dignity and Freedom** invokes the values of the State of Israel as a Jewish and democratic state.

Thus Jewish law has become officially an important part of the law in Israel. Even previous to these enactments occasional reference to Jewish law was made in the regular court system, mainly by those lawyers and judges knowledgeable of the principles involved.

The religious courts in Israel adjudicate in accordance with their respective religious principles, the Rabbinical courts applying Jewish law. Jewish law has also influenced and entered Israeli law through the process of direct reception and reception by reference.

In the past, Jewish law was exercised as an internal legal system within Jewish communities in those countries where these communities were given judicial autonomy. Today it is sometimes used in voluntary Rabbinic ad hoc tribunals where the parties prefer and agree to be bound by halakhic rulings.

"The term **mishpat ivri**, in its currently accepted meaning, includes only those parts of the Halakhah corresponding to what generally is included in the corpus juris of other contemporary legal systems, namely, laws that govern relationships in human society, and not the precepts that deal with the relationship between people and God."[2]

This article cannot attempt to cover the vast bibliography constituting the literary sources of Jewish law. A brief discussion and a selected list of sources for further reference must suffice.

---

[1] Foundations of law. 1980; 34 L.S.I. 181

[2] Elon. M. Jewish Law:History. Sources and Principles (Jewish Publication Society. 1994). vol.1. p.105

B. PRIMARY SOURCES

1. Bible

The legal and literary sources of Mishpat Ivri include first, the most primary source which is the **Bible** and more specifically, the **Pentateuch (Torah)**, the five books of Moses: Genesis, Exodus, Leviticus, Numbers, Deuteronomy and to a lesser degree, the Books of the Prophets and the Hagiographa. Together these books constitute the Bible (Tanah) also known as the Written Law

2. Mishna

About 200 C.E. the **Mishna** was compiled by Rabbi Judah ha-Nasi and constitutes the post-Mosaic "Corpus Juris" of Jewish law. It was the first code to be compiled after the Written Law and is considered an authoritative statement of the Oral Law.

The Mishna is comprised of six sections or orders (sedarim), each dealing with a general area of law and subdivided into tractates (masekhtot) covering specific topics. Each tractate is made up of chapters, and each chapter contains "mishnayot". The traditional citation refers to tractate abbreviation, chapter and mishna, e.g. Gitt. 3:4; i.e. tractate Gittin, chapter 3, mishna 4. It is assumed that the reader knows to which major order the tractate belongs - in this case Gittin, which deals with divorce, is in the section Nashim (Women).

Most of the legal material in the Mishna is concentrated in two orders - Nashim (Women) and Nezikim (Damages) - although some topics may be found in other sections.

Following is the arrangement of the Mishna in six orders - "sedarim" The subdivision into tractates with their abbreviations is given only for the two orders containing mainly legal topics.

Zeraim - mainly agricultural law
Moed - religious festivals
Nashim (women) - family law
- Yebamoth (levirate marriage), Yeb.
- Ketuboth (marriage contracts), Ket.
- Nedarim (vows), Ned.
- Nazir (nazirite), Naz.
- Sotah (suspected adultress), Sot.
- Gittin (divorce), Gitt.
- Kiddushin (marriage), Kidd.

Nezikin (damages) - civil law, criminal law and procedure
- Baba Kamma (torts), B.K.
- Baba Metzia (civil law), B.M.

Baba Bathra (property law), B.B.
Sanhedrin (judges), Sanh.
Makkoth (flagellation), Makk.
Shevuot (oaths), Shebu.
Eduyot (procedure), Eduy.
Avoda Zara (idolatry), A.Zar.
Avot (ethical maxims)
Horayoth (erroneous rulings of the court), Hor.

Kodashim (law relating to the Holy Temple)
Tohoroth (laws about purity of persons, things, places)[3]

Another book of laws from this period is the **Tosefta** which is similar to the Mishna in many ways while bringing some additional laws; however it is quoted much less . This era gave rise also to compilations of methods of biblical interpretation called **Midrashe halakha** which include the Mekhilta of Rabbi Yishmael and Mekhilta of Shimon Bar Yohai on the book of Exodus, Sifra on Leviticus, Sifre on Numbers and Deuteronomy.

3. Talmud

Two authoritative works followed: the **Jerusalem Talmud** and the **Babylonian Talmud** which commented on and enlarged upon the Mishna. They follow, in general, the order of the tractates as in the Mishna. The Babylonian Talmud is the more authoritative and included "deliberations of the sages...and decisory rules and has been accepted in the halakhic [Jewish legal] world as authentic and binding material constituting the starting point for the deliberation of any [legal] subject whatsoever."[4] Both Talmuds were written in Aramaic and have appeared in many editions in various formats.

4. Commentaries

The **Perushim and Hiddushim** - commentaries and novellae - came next and comprise multitudinous volumes by various scholars who elucidated the earlier sources by adding glosses, explaining passages and reconciling differing views. The classic commentator on both the Bible and the Babylonian Talmud was **Rashi,** Rabbi Shlomo Izhaki, who lived in the 11th century in France. A group of his disciples and grandchildren, known as the **Tosafot,** added comments and novellae.

---

[3] Encyclopedia Judaica, vol.15, 751-752 (Keter, 1971);P.Segal, "Jewish law during the Tannaitic period" in An Introduction to the History and Sources of Jewish law, ed. by N.S.Hecht et al, (Clarendon, 1996)

[4] M. Elon, Principles of Jewish Law (1975).

The **Hiddushim** - novellae - " are a form of interpretation in which the writer does not merely clarify the text, but aims to explain the motives or reasons behind the text, to settle potential contradictions between the text and other sources and to discuss the legal (halakhic) issues that derive from it in a general manner". [5] Important writers from the past include the **Ramban,** Nahmanides - Rabbi Moses ben Nahman and the **Rashba** - R.Solomon ben Abraham Aderet; novellae continue to be written even today by contemporary rabbis.

5. Codifications

Codification of the law followed a long and complex path and mention can be made of only a few of the major works. Following the original primary sources and commentaries, there was a need to digest and apply the whole body of accompanying legal literature, including the commentaries, novellae and responsa. Several major compilations appeared including:

Sefer haHalahot of R. Isaac Alfasi, one of the most important compilations of Jewish law, appeared in the 11th century. In the 12th century Maimonides produced the **Mishnah Torah** which comprised 14 books also known as the Yad Hahazaka which codified the law. This is a major, comprehensive, outstanding work still consulted today. The 14th century saw the appearance of **Piskei haRosh** by R. Asher b. Jehiel. His son R. Jacob ben Asher compiled the work entitled **Arba'ah Turim**, known as the **Tur**, "which appeared first in Spain before 1340, and rose to be the primary restatement of the law for more than 200 years."[6] This work was divided into four major sections and included only laws and practices which were current and in practice in the Diaspora (outside of the land of Israel); the last two sections contain legal matters. The four sections are:

Orah Hayyim - covers religious ritual matters and festivals
Yoreh de'ah - other matters of religious law
Even Ha'ezer - covers marriage and divorce ,
Hoshen Hamishpat - dealing with courts, commerce, torts, homicide, etc.

R. Joseph Karo (also written as Caro) wrote an extensive commentary on the Tur, entitled **Bet Yosef** in the 16th century. However, he is best known for his concise restatement of the practical law, **Shulhan Arukh,**

5 J. Shochetman."Jewish law in Spain and the halakhic activity of its scholars" in An Introduction to the History and Sources of Jewish Law. (ed.N.S.Hecht et al)(Oxford. 1996)

6 S.M.Passamaneck. "Toward sunrise in the East 1300-1565" in Introduction to the History and Sources of Jewish Law. (ed. N.S.Hect et al)(Oxford. 1996)

which is the authoritative codex of Jewish law even today. He used the format of the four sections of the Tur and presented a digest of the previous authorities. The Shulhan Arukh was fairly easy to use and understand and together with the glosses of R. Moses Isserles - the Mappah - became the standard law code; it became very popular for a quick answer on a point of law. It was printed for the first time in 1565 in Venice and has since gone through many editions and some translations. Since this work there has been no other codification of such breadth and authority; rather, later Rabbinic jurists prepared commentaries upon it.

6. Responsa

The **She'elot u'Teshuvot** - responsa literature - may be viewed as the body of case law of the Jewish legal system. These are compilations of questions posed by local judges to famous scholars or leading Rabbis for their authoritative and reasoned decisions. They reflected the legal reality of each era with its personal, communal, commercial and criminal problems and disputes. There are hundreds of such works covering centuries of Rabbinic rulings in varied countries. The more important responsa rulings were subsequently incorporated into the major codifications. Outstanding among the respondents include the Rosh - Rabbi Asher, the Rashba and Rabbi Meir of Rothenburg

Bar-Ilan University, Responsa project. Bar-Ilan sponsors an ongoing project of computer based information retrieval of selected responsa literature. This literature contained vast information but was unorganized and virtually unindexed, making systematic research extremely difficult. The project gathered many volumes of responsa from various centuries and countries and committed them to digital format. This project has added to its database the main literary sources of Judaism discussed above: Bible, Mishna, Talmuds, Maimonides and other classic commentators. This is an outstanding and comprehensive collection of Judaica materials dating back hundreds of years which have been collected, organized and made digitally accessible by the Bar Ilan University Computer Center. Published in cd-rom format, it contains numerous works of Jewish Law and has become an essential research tool. Although originally including only responsa it has since been enlarged to encompass almost all of the main works of Jewish law. In addition to the "primary" materials it comprises hundreds of commentaries ranging from the classic commentators, later Rabbis through the ages and continuing to modern times. Its full text search engine is very well developed to take into account the numerous variations of words in the Hebrew grammar. It was the first CD-Rom and

search engine produced in Israel and was a world leader in creating the algorithms of full text searching, first appearing in the early 1970's.

Its contents include:

Bible
Commentaries on the Bible
Mishna
Tosefta
Babylonian Talmud
Rashi"s commentary on the Talmud and Tosfot
Jerusalem Talmud
Midrashei halakha
Midrashei agadda
Zohar
Rambam (Maimonides)
Tur
Bet Yosef
Shulhan Arukh (Code of law by Joseph Karo) and commentaries
Responsa - all generations of respondents to contemporary times.

(Version 7, 1999. Produced by Bar Ilan University, Responsa Project, Ramat Gan).

Following is a selected bibliography of basic materials which may serve as a start for a law library endeavoring to assemble a collection of Jewish law. Works in English are listed wherever possible.

C. BIBLIOGRAPHY

1. PRIMARY SOURCES

Bible

The Bible appears in untold editions in the original Hebrew, with or without commentaries, as well as translations into virtually every language.

Mishna

Danby, Herbert. **The Mishnah**. Oxford University Press, 1933. A scholarly translation in English.

Mishnayoth. 2d ed. by Philip Blackman. New York, Judaica Press, 1964. 6v. Includes commentaries.

Talmud

Talmud Bavli. The Gemara: the classic Vilna edition, with an annotated, interpretive elucidation, as an aid to Talmud study. Elucidated by a team of Torah scholars under the general editorship of H. Goldwurm and N. Scherman. Schottenstein edition. Artscroll series. Brooklyn, Mesorah Publications, 1990. Hebrew text and English translation and commentaries. Useful work for the English speaker.

The Talmud. The Steinsaltz edition. Commentary by Adin Steinsaltz. New York, Random House, 1989. Includes the Hebrew and Aramaic texts of the Talmud and Rashi's commentary. Not yet complete

The Babylonian Talmud, ed. by I. Epstein. English translation. London, Soncino, 1938. 18v.

Responsa

Bar Ilan University Responsa Project. See above section on responsa

Bazak, J. Jewish law and Jewish life - selected rabbinical responsa. Translated by S.M. Passamaneck. N.Y., Union Am. Heb. Congregations, 1977. 4v.

Death and euthanasia in Jewish law- essays and responsa. Edited by Walter Jacob and M. Zemer. Pittsburgh, Freehof Inst. of Progressive Halakhah, 1994.

Deutsch, Sinai. Legal services to judges and lawyers by the Bar Ilan University computer program on rabbinical responsa. in Law in Multicultural Societies (IALL meeting, Jerusalem, 1985) pp.83-95

Feinstein, Moshe (Rabbi). Responsa of Rav Moshe Feinstein. Translation and commentary by Moshe D. Tendler. Hoboken, Ktav, 1996.

Finkel, A. The responsa anthology. Aronson, 1990.

Freehof, Solomon. The responsa literature and a treasury of responsa. N.Y. Ktav, 1973 (Reprint).

Hurwitz, Simon. The responsa of Solomon Luria (Maharshal). The legal decisions of the famous 16th century sage. N.Y., Bloch, 1968.

Jakobovitz, Immanuel. Jewish law faces modern problems. N.Y. Yeshiva Univ., 1965.

Litvin, Baruch. Jewish identity; modern responsa and opinions on the registration of children of mixed marriages. David Ben-Gurion's query to leaders of world Jewry: a documentary compilation. Edited by Sidney B. Hoenig. New York, Feldheim, 1970.

Shulhan Arukh

Appel, Gersion. The concise code of Jewish law. Compiled from Kitzur Shulhan Aruch and traditional sources. New York, Ktav, 1977

Karo, Joseph. The traditional Jewish law of sale; Shulhan Arukh, Hoshen Mishpat, Chapters 189 – 240. Translated and annotated by Stephen M. Passamaneck. Cincinnati, Hebrew Union College, 1983.

Ganzfried, Solomon. Code of Jewish law, kitzur shulhan arukh by Joseph Caro. Trans. by Hyman E. Goldin. Rev. ed. New York, Hebrew Pub. Co., 1961. 4v. Deals mainly with ritual matters

---Kitzur Shulchon Oruch; the classic guide to the everyday observance of Jewish law. A new translation with notes and diagrams by Eliyahu Touger. New York, Moznaim, 1991 2v.

Quint, Emanuel. A restatement of rabbinic civil law. Jerusalem Institute of Jewish Law. Northvale, N.J., J. Aronson, 1990-1995, 7v. Vol.1 - Laws of judges, evidence; Vol. 2 - Laws of loans; Vol. 3 - Laws of pleading; Vol. 4 - Laws of collection of debts, collection from heirs, mortgages, agency, guarantee, presumption of ownership of personality; Vol. 5 - Laws of presumption of ownership of realty, injuries to neighbors, joint ownership of realty, partition of realty; Vol. 6 - Laws of partnerships, agents, sales, acquisition of personality; Vol.7 -Discrepancies in sales, gifts of a healthy person, gifts causa mortis.

This is an ambitious attempt at a restatement of part four, Hoshen HaMishpat, of the Shulhan Arukh by R. Joseph Karo. The goal of the Jewish Institute of Law is to state clearly and precisely the Jewish law in light of Rabbinic decisions, principles and rules.

Cases

Rabbinical Courts of Israel. Piskei din Rabbaniim. Decisions of the Rabbinical Courts. Vol. 1, 1953 - [v.18,1998]. For further information on Rabbinical Courts and judgments see Chapter 4, section G, dealing with religious courts and reports.

Bet ha-Din le-Dinei Mamonot ule-Virur Yahadut. Special court of the Chief Rabbinate applying Jewish Law to civil matters. Jerusalem.Vol.1, 1993 – [v.6,1999]

Bet ha-Din ha-Ezori le-Dinei Mamonot. Special Rabbinic court in Kiryat Arba-Har Hevron applying Jewish Law. 1995-

Yisraeli, Sha'ul. Sefer mishpat Sha'ul; piskei din asher nadonu bevait hadin hagadol beYerushalayim. Jerusalem, Yeshivat Eretz Chemda. 1997- . Cases dealt with by the Rabbinic tribunal.

Other

Yale Judaica Series, consists mainly of translations of ancient and medieval Jewish classics from Hebrew, Aramaic, Ethiopic, or Arabic. An important part of the Series is the extensive but not complete translation of **The Code of Maimonides.**

2. REFERENCE WORKS

Encyclopedia Judaica. Scholarly work on topics related to Jews and Judaism. Has many articles on areas of Jewish Law. These were collected and printed in a work edited by M. Elon (see infra). Jerusalem, Keter, 1974. 16 volumes and yearbooks.

Encyclopedia Talmudica, a digest of halachic literature and Jewish law. Rabbi Herzog World Academy, 1969. Four volumes of the English edition have appeared . The Hebrew edition has 23 volumes since beginning of publication in 1947. A new edition was begun in 1973 but only one volume has appeared.

Rakover, Nahum. The multi-language bibliography of Jewish law. Jerusalem, Jewish Legal Heritage Society, 1990. Excellent, comprehensive work.

---- Otzar hamishpat ; a bibliography of Jewish law, modern books, monographs and articles in Hebrew. Jerusalem, Fischel Institute for Research in Jewish Law, 1975.

Reshimat ma'amarim b'madaei hayahadut (**RAMBI**) [List of articles in Judaica]. Published by the editors of **Kiryat Sepher**. Jerusalem, Magnes Press, no. 1, 1966-. Added title page, introduction, table of contents and index in English. Data available on the web from 1984.

Sarei ha'eleph, a millenium of Hebrew authors (500-1500 C.E.) - a complete bibliographical compendium of Hebraica. Ed. by M.M. Kasher and J.B. Mandelbaum. New York, American Bibliographical Society, 1959. Added title page and short introduction in English.

Weisbard, Phyllis H. Jewish law; bibliography of sources and scholarship in English. Compiled by Phyllis Weisbard, David Schonberg; with a foreword by M. Elon. Littleton, Co., Rothman, 1989.

3. MONOGRAPHS

a. English

Basri, Ezra. Ethics of business finance and charity according to Jewish law. Trans. By E. Touger. Jerusalem, Haktav Inst., 1987. 6 v.

Ben-Menachem, Hanina. Selected topics in Jewish law. Edited by Hanina Ben-Menachem and Neil S. Hecht. Ramat Aviv, Open University of Israel; Boston Univ. School of Law, Institute of Jewish Law, 1987, 2v.

Biale, Rachel. Women and Jewish law; an exploration of women's issues in halakhic sources. New York, Schocken, 1984.

Breitowitz, Irving. Between civil and religious law - the plight of the aguna in American society. Greenwood Press, 1993.
Broyde, Michael. The pursuit of justice and Jewish law - halakhic perspectives on the legal profession. N.Y., Yeshiva Univ. Press, 1998.
Bulka, Reuven P. Jewish marriage; a halakhic ethic. New York, Ktav, 1986.
Cohen, Arnold. An introduction to Jewish civil law. Jerusalem, Feldheim, 1991.
Cohen, Boaz. Jewish and Roman law. New York, Jewish Theological Seminary, 1966. 2v.
Cohn, Haim H. Human rights in Jewish law. New York, Institute of Jewish Affairs, 1984.
--- Jewish law in ancient and modern Israel; selected essays. New York, Ktav, 1971.
--- Selected essays. Edited by Aharon Barak, Ruth Gabizon. Tel Aviv, Bursi Publ. House. 1991. General essays on law with one section containing eight articles on Jewish law
Contemporary legal issues; Jewish law and American law. Edited by Joseph B. Stern. Brookline, Mass., Hebrew College. Milender Institute of Jewish Ethics, 1983. (six source books)
Crime and punishment in Jewish law , essays and responsa. Edited by Walter Jacob and Moshe Zemer. Providence, Berghahn Books, 1999.
Daube, David. Ancient Jewish law; three inaugural lectures. Leiden, E.J. Brill, 1981.
--- Collected works of David Daube. Edited by Calum Carmichael. Berkeley, Univ. of California School of Law, 1992.
---Studies in Biblical law. New York, Ktav, 1969
Elon, Menachem. Jewish law: history, sources, principles. Translated from the Hebrew by M.J. Sykes. Philadelphia, Jewish Publication Society, 1994. 4v.
--- Jewish law (Mishpat Ivri) cases and materials. N.Y., M.Bender, 1999. Excellent teaching tool.
--- Principles of Jewish law. Jerusalem, Keter, 1975. Collection of articles which appeared in Encyclopedia Judaica (Jerusalem, Keter, 1974. 16v. and yearbooks)
Englard, Izhak. Religious law in the Israel legal system. Jerusalem, Hebrew University, Sacher Institute, 1975.
Falk, Ze'ev W. "Jewish family law" Int'l Ency. Comp.Law.Vol.4, ch.11.
--- "Jewish law" in Derrett, J. An introd. to legal systems, 1968.
--- Law and religion; the Jewish experience. Jerusalem, Mesharim, 1981
Golding, Martin P. Jewish law and legal theory. New York, New York U.P., 1993.

Halakhah and Mishpat HaMelukhah. Collection of articles in Hebrew and English dealing with Jewish law and the civil state. Jewish Political Studies Review, Vol. 10, no.3/4, 1998.

Haut, Irvin H. Divorce in Jewish law and life. New York, Sepher-Hermon, 1983.

Hecht, N.S. [et al]. An introduction to the history and sources of Jewish law. Oxford, Clarendon Pr., 1996.

Herzog, Isaac. The main institutions of Jewish law. London, Soncino, 1965. 2v.

--- Judaism; law & ethics. Essays by Isaac Herzog, selected by Chaim Herzog. London, Soncino, 1974.

International Seminar on the Sources of Contemporary Law (lst; 1983, Jerusalem). Jewish law and current legal problems. Edited by Nahum Rakover. Jerusalem, The Jewish Legal Heritage Society, 1984.

International Seminar on the Sources of Contemporary Law (2d; 1985, Jerusalem). Maimonides as codifier of Jewish law. Ed. N. Rakover,1987.

International Seminar on the Sources of Contemporary Law (3d., 1997, Jerusalem) Law and the Noahides. Ed. N. Rakover.

Jackson, Bernard, S. Jewish law in legal history and the modern world. Leiden, E.J. Brill, 1980.

--- Modern research in Jewish law. Leiden, E.J.Brill, 1980

Jewish Law in Context: authority, process and method; studies in Jewish law. Ed. By H. Ben-Menachem, N. Hecht. Harwood Academic Pub., 1998.

Jewish Legal Writings by Women. Edited by M.D. Halpern and Chana Safrai. Jerusalem, Urim, 1998.

Kirschenbaum, Aaron. Equity in Jewish law. Hoboken, Ktav, 1991.

Konvitz, Milton . Torah and constitution; essays in American Jewish thought. Syracuse, N.Y., Syracuse U.P., 1998

Levine, Aaron. Economic public policy and Jewish law. Hoboken, Ktav, 1993

--- Free enterprise and Jewish law; aspects of Jewish business ethics. New York, Ktav, 1980.

--- Judaism and human rights. New York, W.W.Norton, 1972.

Medicine and Jewish law. Edited by Fred Rosner. Northvale, N.J., J. Aronson, 1990.

Meiselman, Moshe. Jewish woman in Jewish law. New York, Ktav, 1978

Mendelson, Samuel. The criminal justice of the Jews. With new introd. by Irwin Haut. N.Y., Sepher-Hermon Press, 1991.

Mielziner, Moses. Introduction to the Talmud. New York, Block Pub. Co. 1968

--- Jewish law of marriage and divorce in ancient and modern times, and its relation to the law of the state. Cincinnati, Block, 1984.

Neusner, Jacob. A history of the Mishnaic law of damages. Leiden, E.J.Brill, 1983, 2v.

--- Jewish law from Moses to the Mishnah (lectures on religion). Atlanta, Scholars Press, 1998.

Newman J. Halachic sources from the beginning to the 9th century. Leiden, E.J. Brill, 1969.

Novak, David. Natural law in Judaism. Cambridge Univ. Press., 1998

Passamaneck, Stephen M. Insurance in rabbinic law. Edinburgh U.P., 1974.

---- Traditional Jewish law of sale, Shulkhan Arukh Hoshen Mishpat, chap.189-240. Translated and annotated. Cincinnati, Hebrew Union College Press, 1983.

Quint, Emanuel. Jewish jurisprudence; its sources and modern applications. By Emanuel B. Quint and Neil S. Hecht. Chur, Switzerland, Harwood Academic Publ., 1980, 2v.

Rackman, Emanuel. Modern halakhah for our time. Hoboken, N.J., Ktav, 1996

Rakover, Nahum. A guide to the sources of Jewish law. Jerusalem, Library of Jewish Law, 1994.

--- Modern applications of Jewish law; resolution of contemporary problems according to Jewish sources in Israeli courts. Jerusalem, Ministry of Justice, Jewish Legal Heritage Society, Foundation for the Advancement of Jewish Law, 1993. 2v.

Riskin, Shlomo. Women and Jewish divorce; the rebellious wife, the agunah and the right of women to initiate divorce, a halakhic solution. Hoboken, N.J., Ktav, 1989.

Roth, Sol. Halakhah and politics; the Jewish idea of the state. New York, Ktav, 1988.

Schiffman, Lawrence Harvey. Sectarian law in the Dead Sea scrolls; courts, testimony and the penal code. Chico, Scholars Press, 1983.

Schimmel, Harry C. The oral law; a study of the Rabbinic contribution to Torah She-be-al-peh. Jerusalem, Feldheim, 1973.

Silberg, Moshe. Talmudic law and the modern state. Translated by Ben Zion Bokser; edited by Marvin S. Wiener. New York, Burning Bush Pr., 1973.

Studies in Jewish Jurisprudence. N.Y., Hermon Press, 1971- . 5v.

Tamari, Meir. With all your possessions; Jewish ethics and economic life. New York, Free Press, 1987.

Twersky, Isadore. Introduction to the Code of Maimonides (Mishneh Torah) New Haven, Yale U.P., 1980 (Yale Judaica series; v.22)

Weisfeld, Israel H. Labor legislation in the Bible and Talmud. New York, Yeshiva U.P., 1974.
Zipperstein, Edward. Business ethics in Jewish law. N.Y., Ktav, 1983.
Zohar, Noam. Alternatives in Jewish bioethics. Albany, SUNY Press, 1997.
(**note** - there are very many articles appearing in periodicals and collections of essays which deal with the various aspects of Jewish law. Therefore, use should be made of periodical indexes in addition to this list, e.g. Index to Jewish Periodicals, Index to Legal Periodicals in Israel)

3. Monographs
b. Hebrew
(Due to the multitudinous number of books on this subject only a few selected, representative studies are listed)

Albeck, Shalom, Dinei hamamanot ba-Talmud. The law of property and contract in the Talmud. Tel-Aviv, Dvir, 1976.
--- Mavo le-mishpat ha-ivri beyemai ha-Talmud. Introduction to Jewish Law in Talmudic Times. Ramat Gan, Bar Ilan University, 1999.
--- Yesodot ha-aveira bedinei HaTalmud. Ramat Gan, Bar-Ilan, University,1997.
Basri, Ezra. Dine mamonot. Ethics of business, finance and charity according to Jewish law. R. Mass, 1974. 6v.
Elon, Menachem. Mishpat ha'ivri: Jewish law, history, sources, principles. 3d ed. Jerusalem, Magnes Press, Hebrew University, 1998. 3v.
Enker, Arnold and S. Deutch, eds. Iyunim bamishpat ha-ivri ubehalakha. Studies in Jewish law - papers presented at the Lublin Conference on Jewish Law. Ramat Gan, Bar-Ilan University, 1998
Goldberg, Yosef. Heskem mamon. Jerusalem, Rabbinic Courts,Shaar Mishpat Inst.,1996. Instructions for drafting contracts in Jewish law.
Gulak, Asher. Yesodei hamishpat ha'ivri. Foundations of Jewish law. Tel-Aviv, Dvir, 1967. 4 pts. in 2v.
Keter - Mekhkarim becalcala umishpat al pi hahalacha. Studies in Economics and law according to the halacha. Kedumim, Keter Institute, v.1, 1996-
Lifshitz, Berachyayu. Asmachta. Promise - obligation and acquisition in Jewish law. Jerusalem, Magnes, 1988.
Medinat Yisrael kemedina yehudit vedemokratit. The State of Israel as a Jewish and democratic state. Colloquium. M.Shamgar, A. Barak, M. Elon et al. Edited by Ron Margolin. World Union for Jewish Studies, 1999.

Mekhkarim bahalakha ubamakhshevet yisrael. Studies in halakha and Jewish thought presented to Rabbi Prof. M. Emanuel Rackman. Edited by Moshe Beer. Bar Ilan University, 1994.

Rakover, Nahum. Hamishpat ha-ivri bakhakikat haKnesset. Jewish law in the debates [and laws] of the Knesset. Ministry of Justice, Jewish Legal Heritage Society, 1988. 2v.

---- Hamishpat ha-ivri bapsikat batei hamishpat beyisrael. Jewish law in the Israeli courts. Ministry of Justice, 1989. 2v.

---- Hamiskhar bamishpat ha-ivri.Commerce in Jewish law. Ministry of Justice, 1987. Chapters on the protection of the consumer, the merchant and the creditor.

--- HaRambam ve-hahok bamedinat Yisrael. Dine mamonot. . Maimonides and the law in Israel . Ministry of Justice. 1985.

--- Hashlikhut vehaharshaa bamishpat ha-ivri. The Jewish law of agency in legal procedings. Rav Kook Inst., 1972.

---- Sidrat mekhkarim veskirot bamishpat ha-ivri. Israel Ministry of Justice. Studies on various topics in Jewish law; series of researches and surveys. Jerusalem. No. 1, 1969. Each issue deals with a separate subject and has its own author.

Shinover, Zvi and Y. Goldberg. Aikhut hakhaim vehasviva. Quality of life and the environment in Jewish sources. Mofet, 1994.

Warhaftig, Shillem. Dine avoda bamishpat ha-ivri. Labor law in Jewish law. Hebrew Univ., 1969. 2v (reprint 1982)

--- Dine hozim. Law of contracts. H. Fishel Inst., 1974

--- Dine matbeah. Law of currency. Jerusalem, Ariel, 1980.

--- Dine miskhar bamishpat ha-ivri. Laws of commerce. Hebrew Univ., 1990

Warhaftig, Zerach. Hahazaka bamishpat ha-ivri. Rav Kook Inst., 1964

--- Huka le-yisrael - dat umedinah. A constitution for Israel - religion and state. Mesilot, 1988

--- Mehkarim bamishpat ha-ivri. Studies in Jewish law. Bar Ilan University, 1985.

Yahadut pnim vehutz. Judaism – a dialogue between cultures. Edited by A.Sagi, D.Schwartz, Y.Z.Stern. Jerusalem, Magnes Press, 1999.
Essays dealing with political thought, Zionism, law and halacha, Judaism and modernity.

(**note** - There are numerous articles dealing with the various aspects of Jewish law; therefore, use should be made of periodical indexes in addition to this list, e.g. Reshimat Maamarim Bemadaei Hayahadut, Index to Legal Periodicals in Israel, etc.).

4. PERIODICALS

Dine Israel, an annual of Jewish law and Israeli family law. Edited by Ze'ev Falk and Aaron Kirschenbaum. Tel-Aviv University, Faculty of Law. Volume 1, 1969- . Articles mainly in Hebrew with small English section.

Jewish Law Annual. Ed. B.S. Jackson. Leiden, Brill. v.1,1978-. English.

Jewish Law Association Studies. Atlanta, Scholars Press. Volume 1, 1985- . English

Jewish Law Report. Edited by Chaim Povarsky, Huntington, N.Y.Touro College. Institute of Jewish Law, 1989- . English

Journal of Halacha and American Law. Surfside, Fl.,Center for Halacha and American Law, Vol.1, 1998- .

Journal of Halacha and Contemporary Society. N.Y., Yeshiva Rabbi Jacob Josef. Vol.1, 1981- .

National Jewish Law Review. N.Y., Nat'l Jewish Students Network. Volumel, 1986-Volume 5, 1990/91. Ceased publication.

Shnaton haMishpat ha-Ivri, annual of the Institute for Research in Jewish law. Jerusalem, Hebrew University. Volume 1, 1974- . Articles in Hebrew. Added title page and table of contents in English.

Techumin, research articles concerning Torah, society and state. annual.Volume 1, 1979- . Hebrew.

There are a number of other periodicals dealing mainly with Judaica which publish, from time to time, articles on the legal aspects of Jewish law, e.g. Noam, Sidra, Sinai, Tarbiz, Torah u-Medina, Torah sh-baal peh, etc.

CHAPTER 10 : PRE-STATE MATERIALS

A. OTTOMAN PERIOD

As was noted in Chapter 1, remnants of the Ottoman and Mandate administrations are present in the current body of law of the State of Israel. The Ottomans ruled Palestine from 1517 to 1917. "Under the Ottoman administration the territory had no legislative or executive bodies elected or appointed to govern it as a distinct political or administrative unit...the territory...was actually ruled autocratically by several Turkish governors, each of whom was in practice the law unto himself who ruled the inhabitants of his district with a hand of iron." (B.Joseph, British Rule in Palestine, p.4, 1948).

An official version of the Ottoman laws was not published in Palestine. In the era of Turkish rule there were no particular difficulties as the authorities turned to Turkish sources; in the Mandate period and after the establishment of the State, however, there were many difficulties due to the fact that very few people understood Turkish and there were no official translations.

The main collection of Ottoman civil law is contained in the Mejelle which is, in effect, a collection of the Moslem religious law concerning civil matters. The Mejelle is divided into sixteen books and is headed by an introduction which states the general rules of law. Each book deals with one central subject, e.g., book of sales.

In Turkey, the Mejelle was repealed more than fifty years ago, although parts of it continued in force in Israel until 1984 when the Repeal of the Mejelle Law, 5744 was passed. The explanatory remarks accompanying the bill note that following the enactment of the law, Foundations of the Law in 1980 which, among other sections, cancelled the obligation to refer to English law, the repeal of the Mejelle completes the cancellation of the mandatory reliance on foreign law in Israel. From now on Israeli law will be based in theory and in practice on original Israeli legal thought.

It should be noted that by repealing the Mejelle there is no intention to uproot any custom which has become a legal source. Despite this act, however, some parts of the Mejelle will remain in force because some laws passed to replace the Mejelle give specific instructions to maintain Ottoman law in certain instances and relating to those agreements made previously.

1.TRANSLATIONS

Mejelle or Mejelle Ahkam il Adliya. Translated by Gad Frumkin. With introduction and notes by the translator. Jerusalem, 1928. 308p.

This is an excellent Hebrew translation by a late Supreme Court justice of the Mandate period. A second edition appeared in 1942 and a third in 1952.

Kovetz hukim Ottomaniim [Collection of Ottoman laws in use in the Land of Israel]. Translated by M. Laniado. Jerusalem, 1929. 361p.

This work, published in Hebrew, includes amendments to the laws by the Mandate government, summaries of Turkish commentators, opinions of French commentators and references to English law.

Kovetz hukim Ottomaniim [Collection of Ottoman laws]. Edited by Shalom Cohen. Tel-Aviv, 1956. 2v.

Volume 1 is a re-issue of the Laniado book with added annotations of decisions of Palestine and Israeli courts, 1920-1954. Volume two contains translations of twelve Ottoman land laws into Hebrew. There are appended translations into English by R.C.Tute and into French by George Young.

Corps de Droit Ottoman. Perhaps the most important translation of Ottoman Laws , in French ,by George Young. (Oxford, Clarendon Press, 1905-06). This seven volume work is considered semi-official but includes laws only up to 1905.

The civil laws of Palestine and Trans-Jordan. Jerusalem, 1933-36. 2v. Unofficial translation into English by Charles A. Hooper.

Translations of various specific laws include the following:
Tute, R.C. **Ottoman land laws with a commentary on the Ottoman land** code. Jerusalem, 1927. 207p. (English).

Ben-Shemesh, A. **Hukei Hamekarkaot** [Land law in the State of Israel]. Tel-Aviv, Masada, 1953. 394p. (Hebrew).

Doukhan, Moshe. **Dinei karkaot** [Land law in the State of Israel]. Jerusalem, 1952. 551p.

The Ottoman land law was in force in Israel as recently as 1969 when it was replaced by a new land law passed by the Knesset.

The Ottoman element of Israeli law does not include decisions as none were published in Palestine under that administration and that legal system does not recognize the theory of precedent.

B. MANDATE PERIOD

The British administration in Palestine started with the military conquest and occupation by the British Armed Forces headed by General Allenby in 1917. Not until 1922 did Palestine become a British mandate by authorization of the League of Nations, which used the mandate system for areas which were deemed unprepared for independence. As previously mentioned, the Mandate for Palestine declared, inter alia, that it was "in favor of the establishment in Palestine of a national home for the Jewish People" in accordance with the Balfour Declaration of 1917. From a legal viewpoint, the Mandate gave Great Britain governmental authority in Palestine and, theoretically, this authority was limited by the Mandate, but in practice it was applied as in a British colony.

Great Britain did not act through its Parliament but rather directly through the local administration in Palestine . Legislative authority was vested in two bodies, the King and the High Commissioner, who was appointed by the government in London. The King exercised his authority infrequently via the Order-in-Council; e.g., Palestine Order-in-Council, 1922 which established the legal structure, sources and court jurisdictions of the new mandate.

Regular legislation emanated from the High Commissioner in the form of ordinances. The term "acts" was reserved for acts of Parliament. In effect, the High Commissioner was both legislative and administrative head with no real separation between those powers; his declarations took the form of ordinances or regulations and the distinction between them was not always clear. Subsidiary legislation consisted of various categories, e.g., regulations, rules, orders, public notices and proclamations.

The Order-in-Council of 1922 established the normative sources of law. According to its paragraph 46, the main sources of law are:

1. The Ottoman law in force in Palestine on November 1, 1914, as long as it was not repealed or superseded by the Mandate government. The Mandate administration did not choose to alter Ottoman law, especially the Mejelle, which was Moslem religious law, and the land law which is one of the most complicated systems extant. It sought to make no drastic changes in areas already having a more or less orderly and logical

arrangement. In addition, they were reluctant to repeal written legislation and replace it with doctrines of precedent and common law.

2. Mandate legislation. The Mandate laws modernized the Ottoman system especially in the areas of the commercial law, criminal law and court procedure.

3. Doctrines of common law and equity were to be referred to in the event of lacunae in the law. In general when the law in a certain subject was unclear under the Turkish system and there was no Mandate law, reference was made to English law. Theoretically, the use of English case law was limited to areas in which conditions existing in Palestine resembled those in England but in practice, the courts turned to English law when they preferred the results obtained there; this was especially true in cases which might rely on an Ottoman law which had already been repealed in Turkey. Thus, much reference to English law was made and the common law has greatly influenced Israeli law.

1. LEGISLATION and COLLECTIONS OF LEGISLATION

The British instituted a gazette publication system as existed in all her colonies and mandates. The history of this series in Palestine follows.

Official Gazette (Occupied Enemy Territory Administration) (South)

It included legislation of the military occupation government which administered the area between October 1917 and June 1920. This legislation was absorbed into the Mandate law. The ordinances were enacted by the Occupied Enemy Territory Administration, the Egyptian Expeditionary Force and the Military Governors of Palestine. This collection is of limited importance due to the fact that those laws which were still in effect in 1934 were included in the collection of laws in force compiled by Drayton (see infra).

Official Gazette of the Government of Palestine (O.G.)

All legislative material was published in this gazette from July 1, 1920 to August 1932. In 1920 the gazette was divided into three parts - the gazette itself containing various notices and announcements, supplement one containing ordinances and supplement two containing subsidiary legislation. In 1932 the title changed to the Palestine Gazette.

The Palestine Gazette (P.G.)

It was published from August 25, 1932 until May 14, 1948. Initially it comprised three sections: Palestine Gazette, the main section which published announcements, notices, registration of trademarks and patents;

Supplement 1 - ordinances
Supplement 2 - subsidiary legislation.

The draft bills appeared originally in the main section on blue-colored paper (a custom which continues today). After various changes in sequence, the Palestine Gazette in 1945 included the three sections mentioned above plus
Supplement 3 - draft laws and
Supplement 4 - patents and trademarks.

The main section was issued in consecutively numbered pamphlets which were bound into one or two volumes each year. The supplements were appendices to the main part. Most volumes included an annual index.

The gazette was published in three languages - English, Hebrew and Arabic. The English version is the authoritative one according to section 32 of the Interpretation Ordinance (New Version). Although the volume and pamphlet numbers are identical in all languages the pagination differs. The Hebrew edition carried the title 'Iton Rishmi.

COLLECTIONS OF MANDATE LEGISLATION

Drayton, Robert H. The laws of Palestine. Rev. ed. London, Waterlow, 1934. 3v.

Drayton, a member of the Mandate administration, drafted many laws and was the compiler and editor of this collection of the laws enacted between 1917 and 1933. This compilation was authorized per Revised Edition of the Laws Ordinance (P.G. 1934, Supp.1 at 193). Subsidiary legislation is included only insofar as the compiler saw fit. The work includes a chart of Ottoman laws which had been repealed or amended by Mandate legislation.

Translations into Hebrew and Arabic were published but the English edition is the only official, binding text. Some sections of the law which appear in Drayton are still in force in Israel today.

Of the three volumes of Drayton, volumes one and two are an alphabetical arrangement of the ordinances. Volume three contains three main sections plus an index to the set. One section contains subsidiary legislation, the second rules of court which were established by the senior judge, and the third includes Imperial acts and orders-in-council. Imperial acts are those that were enacted by the Parliament in London for the colonies. Orders-in-Council were established by the King expressly for the Mandate.

In 1937 an ordinance was enacted giving official status to the revision updating Drayton, entitled the **Revised Edition of the Laws (Revision)**

Ordinance (P.G. 1937, Supp. 1, at 1). It listed all amendments to ordinance found in Drayton and recorded new laws.

There are several other unofficial collections of laws:

Bentwich, Norman, comp. Legislation of Palestine, 1918-1925, Alexandria. Printed for the Government of Palestine by Whitehead Morris Ltd., 1926 2v.

This is a collection of all legislation enacted between 1918 and 1925 which was still valid and in force at the end of 1925. Volume one contains ordinances and volume two lists notices; both are arranged in chronological order. This work has a quasi-authoritative status.

Doukhan, Moses. Law of Palestine. Tel-Aviv, Rotenberg, 1932-35. 1918-1925, 2v. 1926-1931, 5v. 1932, 1v. 1933, 1v. 1934/35 2v.

This is an alphabetical arrangement of ordinances, edited and published privately. The volumes covering the years 1926-1931 were published in 1932 supplementing the Bentwich collection. The two volumes covering 1918-1925 were published retrospectively in 1933. Annual supplements appeared for 1932-1935 and Leon Rotenberg compiled the laws for 1933-1935.

Apelbom, A.M. Annotated laws of Palestine. Tel-Aviv, Bursi, 1944.

This was an ambitious attempt to consolidate and annotate all the laws in force in Palestine. It presented a statement of the statute law with annotations of case law in alphabetical arrangement based on Drayton's system. 6v.

Hochman, Moshe. Osef Hukei Yisrael [Collection of the laws of Israel]. Tel-Aviv, 1954. Laws, 7v. loose-leaf. Regulations, 7v. loose-leaf.

Although this set was published after the establishment of the State, it includes Mandate legislation that was still in force in addition to Israeli legislation. The laws appeared in their original language, English for the Mandate period and Hebrew for the State. This was an important set at the time since Drayton was fast becoming obsolete. The arrangement was alphabetical as in Drayton. It was published in two series, the statutes in green binders and the regulations in brown. Publication ceased.

Rabiner. Laws of Israel (Hebrew)

Published in 1953, this set included Ottoman, Mandate and Israeli laws in force. It was arranged by subject and included case annotations. Since it was not kept up to date, it is of little use today.

Bar-Zeev. The lawfinder and annotator. 1v. loose-leaf.

A rare reference tool published near the end of the Mandate period and was useful for finding legislative amendments and repeals. Not supplemented.

2. THE COURTS AND COLLECTIONS OF REPORTS

The court system was divided into two parts (1) civil courts and (2) religious courts. The distinction continues today in the State of Israel although the jurisdiction of the religious courts has been diminished.

Magistrates Court - a court of the first instance with jurisdiction to hear civil cases amounting to less than IL 250 and criminal cases not constituting felonies. Generally only one judge presided.

District Court - authorized to consider civil cases involving more than IL250 and most criminal cases dealing with a felony. This Court also heard appeals from the Magistrates courts.

Due to the complexity of the property law, **Property Courts** were established. Presided over by district court judges who had specialized in property laws, they were discontinued after the establishment of the State.

Criminal Assize Court - a court of first instance in cases where the crime called for the death penalty, e.g., homicide, treason. The judges were appointed from among the District and Supreme Court judges. This court was later abolished. The only instance of the imposition of the death penalty after the establishment of the State was the Eichman trial for which a special court was convened.

Supreme Court - the court of last resort in Palestine. It sat as a supreme court of appeals; however, in civil matters there was a further resort to the **Privy Council** in London, which heard appeals from all British colonies and mandates. The Supreme Court also served as an **Admiralty Court**. Today the District Court in Haifa has this jurisdiction. The Supreme Court additionally sat as a **High Court of Justice**. Over the Court presided the senior judge who, in addition to his function as president of

the court, also was chief in charge of the administration of the courts and even had legislative authority in procedural matters.

RELIGIOUS COURTS

Sec. 51 of the Order-in-Council, 1922, set out the matters considered within the purview of personal status. Sections 52-54 allotted jurisdiction in these matters to the Moslem, Jewish and Christian religious courts respectively. Personal status included all family matters such as annulment, divorce, child and wife maintenance, guardianship, adoption and the "waqf" a type of Arab trust. The Mandate government did not institute any new policy in this area but rather let matters be handled as they had been under the Ottomans. There was a Special Tribunal which convened to adjudicate questions of jurisdiction between the civil and religious courts. After the establishment of the State several matters were removed from religious jurisdiction.

COLLECTIONS OF MANDATE COURT REPORTS

Decisions from the Mandate period are no longer regarded as authoritative in Israel today. Until 1934 court reports were not published regularly. As a matter of fact, they weren't published at all in the early years of the Mandate and access to decisions was possible only with special permission from the Supreme Court to peruse the material in the court archives. In 1926 the Palestine Post commenced publishing selected summaries of court decisions, which were obviously of limited usefulness.

1. Supreme Court

Law Reports of Palestine (P.L.R.). Ed. by Michael McDonnell. London, Waterlow & Sons Ltd., 1934. Vol. 1, 1920-1933; Vol. 2, 1934-1935; Vols. 3-14, 1936-1947 (one volume each year).

These volumes reported selected decisions of the higher courts including the Supreme Court and the Special Tribunal. The first two volumes presented summaries of decisions but in later volumes the full text was given. The set was official and was edited by the senior Supreme Court Justice, Henry E. Baker, and thereafter by Saleem Azouri.

Current Law reports (C.L.R.). Ed. by M. Levanon, Jerusalem. 1937-1942 in 11 volumes. This series reported judgments of the Supreme Court.

Supreme Court Judgments (S.C.J.). Ed. by A.M. Apelbom and H. Kitzinger, Tel-Aviv, Bursi, 1937-1942. (Two volumes appeared for each year but only one in 1937). Title varies, also known as **Annotated Supreme Court Judgments**. This series was continued by Annotated Law Reports.

Annotated Law Reports (A.L R.). Ed. by M. Levanon, A.M. Apelbom, et al. Tel-Aviv, 1943-1947.
This set consolidated and continued Supreme Court Judgments and Current Law Reports in reporting decisions of the Supreme Court.

2. Other Courts

Collection of judgments of the courts of Palestine (C.O.J.). Ed. by L.M. Rotenberg. Tel-Aviv, 1925-38. Vols. 1-6, 1919-1933; Vols. 7-9, 1934-1936.
Alphabetical arrangement by subject of the civil and criminal decisions of the Privy Council, Court of Appeal, High Court, Special Tribunal, District Court, Land Court, etc.

Hamishpat. Ed. By A. M. Apelbom. 1946-1948. 3 v
Collection of decisions of the District Courts of Palestine, written in Hebrew.

Selected Cases of the District Court of Palestine (S.C.D.C.). Ed. by A.M. Apelbom, et al. Tel-Aviv, 1943-1947, 5v.

Law Reports of the District Court in Tel-Aviv. Ed. by A.M. Apelbom, 1937-1941/42. 5v.
Continued by Selected Cases of the District Courts of Palestine.

Haifa Law Reports (H.L.R.). Ed. by Shalom Cohen. Haifa, Jewish Bar Association, 1945-1947. 6v. Stencilled.

Collection of Judgments of the District and Land Courts of Haifa. 1942. Stencilled.

3. Search Tools

Mafteah l'hol psika ... [Index to decisions]. Ginosar, S. Tel-Aviv, Hukei Halaha lema'ase, 1953. 3v. (Hebrew).

Includes introductory survey to the legal literature. Although published after the establishment of the State it covers mainly Mandate decisions.

Digest of cases reported in the law reports of Palestine. Cohen, Shalom. 1940-1944, 2v.; 1945, 1v.

Subject index to the decisions.

Mafteah clali [Index to Mandate judgments]. Cohen, Shalom. 1919-1947, 26 pamphlets. Stencilled.

Detailed index to reported decisions. Within each subject the arrangement is by series of reports.

4. Periodicals

HaMishpat. Ed. by S. Eisenstadt. 1927- 1929. 2v.

Monthly periodical of legal articles. This should be distinguished from the series of reports with the same title. Hebrew. Ceased publication.

APPENDICES

A. JUSTICES OF THE SUPREME COURT and PRESIDENTS OF THE STATE

B. SELECTED BIBLIOGRAPHY OF BOOKS and ARTICLES IN ENGLISH BY SUBJECT

C. LIST OF ABBREVIATIONS IN ENGLISH AND HEBREW

D. DECLARATION OF THE ESTABLISHMENT OF THE STATE OF ISRAEL AND PROCLAMATION

JUSTICES OF THE SUPREME COURT AND THEIR TERMS OF OFFICE

Smoira, Moshe	1948	-	1953 (1948 – president)
Olshan, Izhak	1948	-	1965 (1953 - vice president, 1954 - president)
Dunkelblum, Menachem	1948	-	1951
Cheshin, Shneor Zalman	1948	-	1959 (1954 - vice president)
Assaf, Simcha	1948	-	1953
Agranat, Shimon	1949	-	1976 (1959 - vice president, 1965 - president)
Silberg, Moshe	1948	-	1970 (1965 - vice president)
Goitein, David	1953	-	1961
Sussman, Yoel	1954	-	1980 (1970 - vice president, 1976 - president)
Landau, Moshe	1953	-	1982 (1976 - vice president, 1980 – president)
Berinson, Zvi	1953	-	1977
Witkon, Alfred	1954	-	1980
Cohn, Haim	1958	-	1981 (1980 - vice president)
Manny, Eliyahu	1962	-	1977
Halevi, Binyamin	1963	-	1969
Kister, Izhak	1965	-	1975
Etzioni, Moshe	1970	-	1978
Kahan, Yitzchak	1970	-	1983 (1982 - president)
Shamgar, Meir	1975	-	1995 (1982 - vice president, 1983 - president)
Shershevsky, Ben Zion	1975	-	1977
Asher, Shlomo	1977	-	1980
Ben-Porat, Miriam	1977	-	1988 (1983 - vice president)
Elon, Menachem	1977	-	1993 (1988 - vice president)
Bechor, David	1978	-	1980
Barak, Aharon	1978	- -	(1994 - vice president, 1995 - president)
Beisky, Moshe	1979	-	1991
Levin, Shlomo	1981	- -	(1995 - vice president)
Cohen, Moshe	1981	-	1982
Levin, Dov	1982	-	1995
Cohen, Yehuda	1982	-	1983
Bach, Gavriel	1982	-	1997
Netanyahu, Shoshana	1983	-	1993
Goldberg, Eliezer	1984	-	1998
Chalima, Abraham	1984	-	1989
Maltz, Yaakov	1988	-	1993
Or, Theodore	1989	- -	
Mazza, Eliyahu	1991	- -	
Cheshin, Mishael	1992	- -	
Kedmi, Yaakov	1994	- -	
Zamir, Yitzhak	1994	- -	
Strassberg-Cohen, Tova	1994	- -	
Tal, Tsevi	1994	-	1997
Dorner, Dalia	1994	- -	
Tirkal, Jacob	1996	- -	
Beinish, Dorit	1996	- -	
Englard, Izhak	1997	- -	

PRESIDENTS OF THE STATE

Weizmann, Chaim	1949 - 1952
Ben-Zvi, Itzhak	1953 - 1963
Shazar, Zalman	1963 - 1973
Katzir, Ephraim	1973 - 1978
Navon, Yitzhak	1978 - 1983
Herzog, Chaim	1983 - 1993
Weizmann, Ezer	1993 -

SELECTED BIBLIOGRAPHY OF BOOKS and ARTICLES in ENGLISH

Note: the major works in Israel are in Hebrew and thus not listed here. There are many legal articles in English on the following subjects as well as many other topics, therefore use should be made of periodical indexes.

ADMINISTRATIVE LAW

"Administrative Law". Segal, Z. Introduction to the Law of Israel. Ed. by A. Shapira and K. DeWitt-Arar. Hague, Kluwer, 1995

"Administrative Law". Zamir, I. The law of Israel: general surveys. Ed. by I. Zamir and S. Colombo. Jerusalem, Hebrew University, 1995

BANKRUPTCY LAW

"Insolvency". Keshet, M. Israeli Business Law; an Essential Guide. Ed. by A. Kaplan. The Hague, Kluwer Law International, 1996

"Insolvency Law". Haviv-Segal, I. Introduction to the Law of Israel. Ed. by A. Shapira and K. De-Witt-Arar. Hague, Kluwer , 1995

BIBLIOGRAPHY

"Access to information and legal sources and their translation into European languages in Israel." Snyder, Esther Mann. (In: International Association of Law Libraries Meeting, Jerusalem, July 21-26, 1985. Law in multicultural societies. pp.189-207)

"Guide to Israel legal bibliography". Snyder, Esther Mann. Law Library Journal, Vol. 70, no. 1, Feb. 1977

Israel legal bibliography in European languages. Livneh, Ernst. Jerusalem, Academon, 1965. Hebrew Univ. of Jerusalem. Faculty of Law. Institute for Legislative Research and Comparative Law; No. 7A.

-A bibliography of Israel law in English and other European languages. Wegner, J. R. Jerusalem, The Hebrew Univ. of Jerusalem. Faculty of Law. Institute for Legislative Research and Comparative Law, 1972

-A bibliography of Israel law in English and other European languages, 1972-1979. Wilkenfeld, J. D.. Jerusalem, The Hebrew Univ. of Jerusalem. Faculty of Law. Institute for Legislative Research and Comparative Law, 1979

-A bibliography of Israeli law in European languages. Sanilevici, R. Jerusalem, Hebrew University. Faculty of Law, Harry Sacher Institute,

1985 (Cumulates and updates Wegner's bibliography, 1972 and Wilkenfeld's bibliography, 1979) (Supplement 1985-1990, 1991)

-A bibliography of Israeli law in European languages 1990-1995. Bonk, H. Jerusalem, Hebrew Univ. Faculty of Law. Sacher Institute for Legislative Research and Comparative Law, 1998

Index to legal periodicals in Israel, 1976-1996. Ed. Esther M. Snyder; Ass't editor: Batia Razinsky. Ramat Gan, Bar Ilan University, Faculty of Law Library, 1997

Israel – bibliography. Ed. Esther M. Snyder. Preliminary compilation by E. Kreiner. Oxford, Clio, 1985 (World bibliographical series; 58)

"Law libraries in Israel." Esther M. Snyder. International Journal of Law Libraries, vol.3, Nov.1973

"The law library in Israel – problems of legal research in a mixed jurisdiction." E.I.Cuomo. Bibliothek und Recht – International, 1991.

CITIZENSHIP

"Citizenship". Rubinstein, A. Israeli Business Law; an Essential Guide. Ed. by A. Kaplan. Hague, Kluwer, 1996

Citizenship and the state: a comparative study of citizenship legislation in Israel, Jordan, Palestine, Syria and Lebanon. U. Davis. Ithaca Press, 1997.

Israel nationality law. Gouldman, M. D. Jerusalem, Hebrew Univ. of Jerusalem. Faculty of Law. Institute for Legislative Research and Comparative Law, 1970

COMMERCIAL LAW

"The Banking System". Halperin, A. Israeli Business Law; an Essential Guide. Ed. by A. Kaplan. Hague, Kluwer, 1996

"Business Entities, An Overview". KPMG Braude Bavly. Israeli Business Law. Ed. By A. Kaplan. Hague, Kluwer, 1996

"Commercial Law". Lerner, Shalom. Introduction to the Law of Israel. Ed. by A. Shapira and K. DeWitt-Arar. Hague,Kluwer ,1995

"The Companies Ordinance: Proposed New Law" Kaplan, A. and Aronson, A. Israeli Business Law; an Essential Guide. Ed. by A. Kaplan. Hague, Kluwer, 1996

Company promoters. Gross, J. H. Tel-Aviv Univ. Israel Institute of Business Research, 1972

Constraints and compromises: trade policy in a democracy: the case

of the U.S. – Israel free trade area. O. Frenkel. N.Y., Garland, 1990.

"Corporate Law". Procaccia, U. Introduction to the Law of Israel. Ed. by A. Shapira and K. DeWitt-Arar. Hague, Kluwer, 1995

Free trade agreement between the State of Israel and the Republic of Poland. [s.l.] [s.n.] 199-

Insider trading in Israel and England; present law and suggestions for new theories of liability. Yoran, A. Jerusalem, Hebrew University. Faculty of Law. Institute for Legis. Research and Comparative Law, 1972

International public procurement law – the evolution of international regimes on public purchasing. A. Reich. Hague, Kluwer, 1999. Section on Israel

Israeli business law; an essential guide. Kaplan, A. Kluwer, 1996

Israeli business law; an essential guide. Revised edition. Kaplan, A.. Kluwer, 1999. (only minor changes from first edition – most of the articles remain the same)

"Law of Agency". Kaplan, A.. Israeli Business Law; an Essential Guide. Ed. by A. Kaplan. The Hague, Kluwer Law International, 1996

The legal framework of economic activity in Israel. Heth, M.. Published in co-operation with the Bank of Israel by F.A.Praeger, 1967

Legal aspects of doing business in the Middle East. Editor: D. Campbell, Kluwer, 1992, vol. 5, Israel by Rosenberg, G.

Legal instruments embodying the Results of the Uruguay Round of multilateral trade negotiations done at Marrakesh on 15 April 1994. Geneva, Gatt Secretariat, 1994

Liberalizing foreign trade. Ed. By D. Papageorgiou, M.Michaely. Vol.3: The experience of Israel and Yugoslavia / N. Halevi and J. Baruh. Cambridge, Blackwell, 1991

The role of the Free Trade Agreement between Israel and the EEC; the legal framework for trading with Israel between theory and practice. Einhorn, Talia. Baden-Baden, Nomos, 1994 (Thesis PhD)

Split corporatism in Israel. Grinberg, L.L. Albany, State Univ. of New York Pr., 1991

The world trade system after the Uruguay Round; implications for Israel and for the European Union. A. Tovias, U. Wacker, eds. Jerusalem. Hebrew University, Helmut Kohl Inst. for European Studies, 1996

COMPARATIVE LAW

International Congress of Comparative Law (6th: 1962: Hamburg). Jerusalem, Hebrew University, 1962. Contents: Les problemes de la codification a la lumiere des experiences et situations actuelled/G. Tedeschi, Y.Englard.The influence of public law on private ownership of real estate in Israel/A.Hecht.The role of the judge in directing civil proceedings/Y. Sussman.Le droit rural en tant que ius proprium/A. J. Levi.Constitutional trends in states that recently have become independent – Israel/Y. Dror. L'autorite des traites internationaux en droit interne/R. Lapidoth.The individual and his access to international jurisdiction/J.J.Lador-Lederer.

International Congress of Comparative Law (7th: 1966: Uppsala) Jerusalem, Hebrew University, 1966. Contents: The sanction for breach of contract, including anticipatory breach/G.Tedeschi.From one man company to commercial foundation/A.Levi.The protection of notorious marks/Z.Sher.The protection of cinematographic films/Z.Sher.Les conflits de la loi nationale avec les traites internationaux/R.Lapidoth.The parliamentary control over the administration, including the ombudsman/L.Boim.Legal restrictions on the freedom of religion and expression/E.Livneh.Legal restrictions on the freedom of occupation/A.Hecht.The right of return and the problem of the fugitive offender/M.D.Gouldman.Judicial limits of administrative discretion/J.Pelley-Karp.Tax measures designed to encourage investment/A.Lapidoth.Competence des jurisdictions penales israeliennes pour les infractions comises a l'etranger/S.Z.Feller.La societe d'une sole personne/S.Ginossar.[Supp.]

International Congress of Comparative Law (8th: 1970: Pescara). Edited by S.Z.Feller. Jerusalem, Hebrew University, 1970. Contents: Relations entre les etats et les eglises/ I.Englard.The relationship in contemporary legal systems between written and unwritten sources of law/R.Gavison.—What are the initiating agencies and what is their mission in each unification movement?/A.J.Levi.Liability, insurance and social responsibility in torts/E.Livneh.The influence of medical and biological progress on private law//Falk.Type contracts and adhesion contracts/A.Bin-Nun.Execution of foreign civil judgments and criminal sentences/A.Shapira.The suspension and interruption of the employment contract/I.Zamir.L'interpretation de la Constitution/C.Klein.Contemporary trends in the division of legislative functions between the legislature and the executive/A.Barak.—Die begrundung von Verwaltungsbescheiden/H.Klinghoffer.The influence of medical and biological progress on criminal law.L'etat

denecessite/S.Z.Feller.Detention prior to judgment/L.Sebba.The right to counsel/E.Harnon.

International Congress of Comparative Law (9th, 1974, Teheran). Edited by I. Englard. Jerusalem, Hebrew University, 1974. Contents: The control of administrative acts by the ordinary courts – a general report/I. Zamir.To what extent are judicial decisions and legal writings sources of law?/U. Yadin.The validity of clauses excluding or limiting liability/G. Shalev.The legal position of children born out of wedlock/Z. Falk.Taxation of multinational corporations in Israel/A. Yoran (Jurkevitz).Tourism contracts in Israel/D. Kolani.The application of the Warsaw Convention in Israel/E. Margalioth.The protection of human rights in constitutional law in Israel/A. Shapira.Legislation replacing short and medium term custodial sentences – Israel/L. Sebba.The accused's right of compensation for detention prior to an acquittal/D. Bein.The right of silence in Israel/E. Harnon.

International Congress of Comparative Law (10th: 1978: Budapest). Edited by S. Goldstein. Jerusalem, Hebrew University, 1978 Contents: The protection of minors in labour law/I.Zamir.Manufacturer's liability in Israel/ D.Kretzmer.The overburdening of the Supreme Court in Israel/S.Shetreet.Collective dismissal/F.Raday.The protection of minors in labour law/A.Miller.The minimal area of privacy/R.Gavison.Mistake in Israeli criminal law/S.Feller.Non individual criminal liability in Israel/D.Bein.The comparative method in criminology/L.Sebba.

International Congress of Comparative Law (11th: 1982: Caracas). Edited by S. Goldstein. Jerusalem, Hebrew University, 1982 Contents: Is codification an outmoded form of legislation?/U. Yadin.The use of comparative law by the legislator/U. Yadin.The effect of inflation on civil liability in Israel/A.Yoran. Piercing the corporate veil/C.I.Goldwater.Rules of law delineating their own sphere of applicability/A.Shapira.Default and opposition/S.Goldstein.Judicial responsibility/S.Shetreet.The legal regime of cooperatives/S.Ottolenghi.Insider trading/U.Procaccia.Administrative and judicial control of trade unions/F.Raday.Comparative law and international protection of human rights/H.H.Cohn.Role et pouvoirs du Conseil des Ministres/C.Klein.Exemptions for reasons of religion and conscience/C.P.Selah.EnD.gering as a criminal act/S.Z.Feller.The legal position of Israel as a requested state which refuses extradition/S.Z.Feller.Problem of defence by counsel or by the accused himself/E. Harnon.Judicial and legislative solutions to the problems raised by inflation for the law of tort, contracts and unjust enrichment/A.Yoran.

International Congress of Comparative Law (12th, Sydney and Melbourne, 1986). Edited by S. Goldstein. Jerusalem, Hebrew University, 1986. Contents: Limits and promises of international norms and procedures: the transnational protection of human rights/S. Shetreet.The role of public law in private international law/C. Wasserstein Fassberg.Recognition and enforcement of foreign money: judgments in civil and commercial matters/A. Shapira.Execution of judgments and means of enforcement available to ordinary courts/S. Goldstein.Judges' use of their personal knowledge/S. Ottolenghi.Legal nature of collective agreements/R. Ben-Israel.International protection of human rights in Israeli law/S. Shetreet.Withdrawal from attempt/S.Z. Feller and M. Kremnitzer.The consequences of secret monitoring in criminal proceedings/N. Zaltzman.Non-publication of judicial decisions/E.I. Cuomo.

International Congress of Comparative Law (13th: 1990: Montreal). Edited by C. W. Fassberg. Jerusalem, Hebrew University, 1990. Contents: Harmonization of common law and civil law in the private law in the State of Israel/A.M.Rabello.The precontractual process under Israeli law/G.Shalev.International adoptions/P.Shifman.Class actions in Israel/S.Goldstein.Legal persons in Israel/U.Procaccia.Crossborder insolvency in Israeli law/C.W. Fassberg.Copyright/J.Weisman.The constitutional and legal status of freedom of speech. /D.Kretzmer. Constitutional protection against confiscatory taxation/Y.Harary.Misuse of computer technology: is it criminal in Israel?/E.Lederman.Exclusion rules in Israeli legal system/E.Harnon and A.Horowitz.Administrative judges and tribunals in Israel/S.Shetreet

International Congress of Comparative Law (14th, Athens, 1994). Ed. by A. M. Rabello. Jerusalem, Hebrew University, 1994. Contents: Continuity and discontinuity of law in times of social revolution/A. M. Rabello and L. Sebba.The requirement of two witnesses in Jewish law/S. Albeck.The style of legislation: narrative norms and constraining norms/L. Belotsky.The use of comparative law by Israeli courts/R. Sanilevici.The Israeli law of prescription/I. Gilead.Rules for declining to exercise jurisdiction in civil and commercial matters: forum non conveniens, lips pendens/S. Goldstein.Agriculture and the environment/M. Hirsch.Corporate takeovers through public markets/Y. Z. Stern.Banking confidentiality/R. Ben-Oliel.Employees' collective rights in the public sector.Integration of Russian immigrants into the Israeli labour market/H. Bonk.Freedom of religion in Israel/R. Lapidoth and M. Corinaldi.Criteria for the linkage between the act subject to taxation and the taxpayer (nationality, domicile or residence or source of

taxation)/A. Lapidoth.

International Congress of Comparative Law (15th, Bristol, 1998). Ed. by A. M. Rabello. Jerusalem, Hebrew University, 1998. Contents: The place of legal history in the training of comparative lawyers/P. Lerner.Language rights in Israel/S. Navot.-The "gentleman's agreement" in legal theory and in modern practice – Israel/G. Shalev-Tort liability in negligence for pure economic loss/I. Gilead.-Medical experiments on human beings in Jewish and Israeli law/D. Sinclair.-Private international law at the end of the twentieth century: progress or regress?/Rhona Shuz.-Summary judgment proceedings in Israeli law: a critical and comparative analysis/S. Goldstein.-The Unidroit principles of international commercial contracts: harmonization of law - a note on the Israeli perspective/A. Rabello.-Assignment of receivables in the world of modern finance/Shalom Lerner.-Bank transfers/R. Ben-Oliel.-Labor-only contracting/F. Raday.-Israel's basic laws on human rights/D. Kreztmer.-Constitutional limitations on privatization/D. Barak-Erez.-Access to justice as a fundamental right.M.Corinaldi.-Responsibility of a state as a legislator/L. Belotsky.

CONSTITUTION

Apple of gold; constitutionalism in Israel and the United States. Jacobsohn, Gary Jeffrey. Princeton, N.J., Princeton Univ. Pr., 1993

"Constitutional law - Israel." Klein, C.. Constitutional Law, ed.A.Alen. Int'l Encyclopedia of Laws. Kluwer, 1991-

"Constitutional Law." Kretzmer, D.. Introduction to the Law of Israel. Ed. by A. Shapira and K. DeWitt-Arar. Hague, Kluwer, 1995

"Constitutional Law". Maoz, Asher. The Law of Israel: general surveys. Ed. by I. Zamir and S. Colombo. Jerusalem, Hebrew University, 1995

Constitutionalism; the Israeli and American experiences. Ed. By D. J. Elazar. Lanham, Univ. Pr. of America. 1990

Israel's written Constitution – translations of the Declaration of Independence and of the Basic Laws, consolidated and updated, January, 1999. Haifa, A.G. Publ., 1999.

Living without a constitution; civil rights in Israel. Sharfman, Dafna. Armonk, N.Y., M.E.Sharpe, 1993

"The Making of the Israeli Constitution; an Overview". H., Naomi. Israeli Business Law; an Essential Guide. Ed. by A. Kaplan. Hague,

Kluwer , 1996

CONTRACTS

"Contract Law". Shalev, G.. Introduction to the Law of Israel. Ed. by A. Shapira and K. DeWitt-Arar. The Hague, Kluwer, 1995

"Contract Law". Shalev, G.. The law of Israel: general surveys. Ed. by I. Zamir and S. Colombo. Jerusalem, Hebrew University, 1995

Freedom of contract and constitutional law. Colloquium of the International Association of Legal Science held in Jerusalem, September 1994. Ed. by A. Rabello, P. Sarcevic. Jerusalem, Sacher Institute for Legislative Research and Comparative Law, Hebrew Univ. of Jerusalem, 1998 .

Good faith in contract; concept and context. Ed. by Roger Brownsword, Norma J. Hird and Geraint Howells. Aldershot, Dartmouth, 1998. [p189: The effect of the duty of good faith in a previous common law system: the experience of Israeli law; p. 311: The transformation of "good faith" in insurance law by D. Friedmann]

"Law of Contract" Shalev, G.. Israeli Business Law; an Essential Guide. A. Kaplan, Paul Ogden. Hague, Kluwer, 1996

COURTS and JUDGES

"Arbitration Law". Ottolenghi, Smadar. Introduction to the Law of Israel. Ed. by A. Shapira and K. DeWitt-Arar. Hague, Kluwer, 1995

"Civil Procedure". Goldstein, S.. Introduction to the Law of Israel. Ed. by A. Shapira and K. DeWitt-Arar. Hague, Kluwer, 1995

Courts, politics and culture in Israel. M. Edelman. Virginia Univ. Pr., 1994.

Demjanjuk affair. Y. Sheftel, trans. By H. Watzman. London, Gollancz, 1994.

Democracy and the courts. Int'l Colloquium. Hebrew Univ. Faculty of Law, 1999.

Eichmann, Adolf. Judgment. Ministry of Justice, 1992-1995.

The global expansion of judicial power. Tate, Chester Neal; Vallinder, Torbjorn, Edelman, Martin. New York, New York Univ. Pr., 1995 [pp.403-416: Israel by Martin Edelman]

Judgment in Jerusalem; Chief Justice Simon Agranat and the Zionist Century. Lahav, PN.. Berkeley, Univ. of California Pr., 1997

Judicial activism in comparative perspective. Holland, K. M.

London, Macmillan, 1991. [pp. 90-116: Judicial activism in Israel by Gary J. Jacobsohn]

Judicial discretion. Barak, Aharon. New Haven, Yale Univ. Pr., 1989 (translated from the Hebrew)

The judiciary of Israel. 2d ed. Żemach, Y. S. Jerusalem, The Institute of Judicial Training for Judges in Israel, 1998

Justice in Israel; a study of the Israeli judiciary. Shetreet, S.. Dordrecht, M. Nijhoff, 1994

"Law of Evidence". Zaltzman, N.. Introduction to the Law of Israel. Ed. by A. Shapira and K. DeWitt-Arar. Hague, Kluwer, 1995

Judgment in Jerusalem; Chief Justice Simon Agranat and the Zionist Century. Lahav, PN.. Berkeley, Univ. of California Pr., 1997

Judicial activism in comparative perspective. Holland, K. M. London, Macmillan, 1991. [pp. 90-116: Judicial activism in Israel by Gary J. Jacobsohn]

Judicial discretion. Barak, A. New Haven, Yale Univ. Pr., 1989 (translated from the Hebrew)

The judiciary of Israel. 2d ed. Zemach, Y. S. Jerusalem, The Institute of Judicial Training for Judges in Israel, 1998

Justice in Israel; a study of the Israeli judiciary. Shetreet, S.. Dordrecht, M. Nijhoff, 1994

Legal services to judges and lawyers by the Bar Ilan University computer program on rabbinical "responsa". Deutsch, Sinai. (In: International Association of Law Libraries Meeting, Jerusalem, July 21-26, 1985. Law in multicultural societies, pp. 83-95)

Political questions in the courts; a judicial function in democracies, Israel and the United States. Zemach, Y. S. Detroit, Wayne Univ. Pr., 1976

The role of courts in society. Shetreet, S.. Dordrecht, M. Nijhoff, 1988

Tears and laughter in an Israel courtroom. Cheshin, Shneour Zalman. Translated from the Hebrew by C. Kleinerman. Philadelphia, Jewish Publ. Society of America, 1971

The trial of Ivan the Terrible; State of Israel vs. J. Demjanjuk. T Teicholz. N.Y., St. Martins Press, 1990

CRIMINAL LAW

Actio libera in causa in criminal law. Gur-Arie, M.. Jerusalem, Hebrew Univ. Faculty of Law. Institute for Legislative Research and Comparative Law, 1984

The causation and prevention of crime in developing countries. International Course in Criminology (12th : 1962 : Jerusalem) Proceedings edited by I. Drapkin. Jerusalem, Hebrew University, 1963

Crime and criminal justice in Israel; assessing the knowledge base toward the twenty-first century. Ed. by R. R. Friedmann. Albany, State Univ. of N.Y.Pr., 1998

Criminal justice in Israel; an annotated bibliography of English language publications, 1948-1993, Friedman, R. R. Westport, Conn., Greenwood Pr., 1995

"Criminal Law". Bein, D.. The law of Israel: general surveys. Ed. by I. Zamir and S. Colombo. Jerusalem, Hebrew University, 1995

"Criminal Law". Kremnitzer, M.. Introduction to the Law of Israel. Ed. by A. Shapira and K. DeWitt-Arar. Hague, Kluwer, 1995

"Criminal Procedure". Mann, K.. Introduction to the Law of Israel. Ed. by A. Shapira and K.. De-Witt-Arar. Hague, Kluwer, 1995

Criminal statistics in Israel 1949-1961. O. Schmelz and D. Salzman. Jerusalem, Hebrew Univ. Faculty of Law. Institute of Criminology, 1964

Israel studies in criminology. Shoham, S. Tel-Aviv, Gomeh, 1970

Justice for all?: Jews and Arabs in the Israeli criminal justice system. A. Rattner and G. Fishman. Praeger, 1998.

The legal norms of delinquency; a comparative study. Mueller, G. New York, New York Univ. School of Law, Criminal Education and Research Center, 1969

Prevention of crime and the treatment of offenders in Israel. Compiled and edited by R. Geva. Jerusalem, 1995. Presented at the Ninth UN Congress of the Prevention of Crime and the Treatment of Offenders April 29 – May 8, 1995, Cairo, Egypt.

A survey of criminal justice in Israel. Bensinger, G.J. Chicago, Center for Urban Policy, Loyola Univ. of Chicago, 1983

What can a police officer do?; a comparative study: U.S.A. – German Federal Republic – Israel – Italy. New York, New York Univesity. School of Law. Criminal Law Education and Research Center, 1974

"White Collar Crime: Criminal Law in the Business World". Sheinman, D., Negev, Navit. Israeli Business Law; an Essential Guide. Ed. by A. Kaplan. Hague, Kluwer, 1996

ENVIRONMENT

Air quality in Israel; selected topics 1974-75. Jones, K.H. Jerusalem, Environment Protection Service, 1976

The environment in Israel. Ministry of the Environment. Compiled and written by S. Gabbay. Jerusalem, Ministry of Environment, 1994

The environment in Israel; national report to the U.N.Conference on Environment and Development. Israel. Ministry of the Environment. Jerusalem, Ministry of Environment, 1992.

"Environmental law – Israel." R. Laster. Environmental Law, ed.M. Boes. Int'l Encyclopedia of Laws. Kluwer, 1991-

Israel in the Mediterranean ecosystem; Israel national report to the Conference of Coastal States of the Medit. Region for the Protection of the Medit. Sea, Monaco, 9-14 January 1978. D. Greenberg and R. Hellman. Jerusalem, Environment Service, 1978

"Law of the Environment". Tal, A.. Israeli Business Law; an Essential Guide. Ed. by A. Kaplan. Hague, Kluwer, 1996

Our shared environment; Int'l Conference on the Environmental chA.ges facing Egypt, Israel, Jordan and the Palestinian territories, 2d, 1995.

EUROPE

Essays on European law and Israel. Ed. A.M. Rabello. Hebrew Univ., 1996.

European legal traditions and Israel - essays on legal history, civil law and codification, European law, Israeli law. Ed. A. Rabello. Hebrew Univ., 1994.

Euro-Mediterranean agreement establishing an association between the European Communities and their member states of the one part, and the State of Israel of the other part. Israel. Ministry of Foreign Affairs. Jerusalem, Israel Information Center, 1995

Future relations between Israel and the European Communities, some alternatives. M. Hirsch. Tel-Aviv, Bursi, 1996.

Israel and the Common Market. Uri Pierre. Jerusalem, Weidenfeld and Nicolson, 1971

Israel and the EEC; Israel's integration in the economic structure of the European Community. 2d. ed. Cohen, Y.. Jerusalem, Ministry of Industry, Trade and Tourism, 1979

Protocols to the EEC-Israel agreement and other basic texts. Brussels, Office for Official Publ. European Communities, 1993

Towards a new European ius commune - essays on European, Italian and Israeli law. Ed. A.Gambaro, A.M.Rabello. Hebrew Univ., 1999.

FAMILY LAW

After the battering; the struggle of battered women with violence in the family. Naamat. Center for the Prevention of Violence in the Family. Compiled and edited by Ronit Lev Ari, Dafna Boostan; English translation: Lou Kaplan. Tel Aviv, Naamat, 1991

Children's rights and traditional values.Ed. by G. Douglas, L. Sebba. Aldershot, Ashgate. 1998

"Family Law". Rosen-Z., Ariel. Introduction to the Law of Israel. Ed. by A. Shapira and K. DeWitt-Arar. Hague, Kluwer, 1995

Israel and the future United Nations Convention on the Rights of the Child. Ed. by P.E. Veerman. Jerusalem, Israel Branch of Defence for Children International, 1989

Israel children's rights monitor; biannual report. Jerusalem, Defence for Children International. Israel Section, 1992

Divorce with respect; a guide to divorce and divorce mediation in Israel. Zaidel, S.R. Haifa, Divorce With Respect, 1990

Frontiers of family law. Editors: Andrew Bainham, D. Pearl and Ros Pickford. New York, J. Wiley, 1995 [pp. 64-74: A perspective on surrogate motherhood in Jewish and Israeli law by P. Shifman]

"The right to parenthood; surrogacy and frozen embryos." Schuz, Rhona. International survey of family law, 1996, pp.237-256.

GENERAL

A people that dwells A.e; speeches and writings of Y. Herzog. Herzog, Y.. Edited by Misha Louvish. London, Weidenfeld & Nicolson, 1975

Democracy, law and national security in Israel. Hofnung, Menachem. Hampshire, Dartmouth, 1966.

Israel among the nations; international and comparative law perspectives on Israel's 50th anniversary. Ed. by A.E. Kellermann, K.

Siehr, Talia Einhorn. Hague, Kluwer , 1998.

Israel government yearbook. Central Office of Information. Jerusalem, 1950-.

Israel at fifty; the development of the law of Israel: the first 50 years. Guberman, Shlomo. Ministry of Foreign Affairs, 1998. Reprint from the Internet site: http:/www.israel-mfa.gov.il/mfa/israel50/law50.htm

Israel 50 years; a history of documents. W.van der Wolf, Global Law Assoc., 1998.

Israel law and business guide. Kaplan, A.. Kluwer, 1994

Israel yearbook and almanac. Tel Aviv, IBRT Translation/Documentation Ltd., 1995 (Continues: Israel Yearbook)

The law of Israel; general surveys. Edited by I. Zamir, S. Colombo. Jerusalem, Hebrew Univ. Faculty of Law. Sacher Institute for Legislative Research and Comparative Law, 1995

The laws of Israel - an introduction for foreign lawyers and students. J.Har-Paz. Haifa Law Publ., 1987.

The legal fight against anti-semitism – survey of developments. S.J.Roth. Israel Yearbook on Human Rights, 1990-

For collections of essays see chapter on Periodicals and Collections of Essays

GOVERNMENT and the LEGAL SYSTEM

The effect of foreign law on the law of Israel. Friedmann, D.. Jerusalem, Israel Law Review Association, 1975

The government and politics of Israel. Boulder, Co., Westview Pr., 1979.

The foreign policy system of Israel; setting, images, process. Brecher, M. London, Oxford Univ. Pr., 1972

Government in Israel. Freudenheim, Y. Translated from the Hebrew by M. Silverstone and C. I. Goldwater. Dobbs Ferry, Oceana, 1967

The government of the State of Israel; a critical account of its parliament, executive and judiciary. Badi, J.. New York, Twayne, 1963

"History and Sources of Israeli law". Shachar, Y.. Introduction to the Law of Israel. Ed. by A. Shapira and K. DeWitt-Arar. Hague, Kluwer,

1995

How to survey Israeli law; guide to preparation for the written bar examinations of the Israel Chamber of Advocates. Bardin, D.. 4th ed. by R. E. Laster. Jerusalem, 1973

"Institutional Organization of the Israeli Legal System". Maoz, Asher. Introduction to the Law of Israel. Ed. by A. Shapira and K.DeWitt-Arar. Hague, Kluwer, 1995

Introduction to the law of Israel. Shapira, Amos and DeWitt-Arar, K. C. The Hague, Kluwer Law International, 1995

"Introduction to the Legal System". Caspi, Z. Israel Business Law; an Essential Guide. Ed. by A. Kaplan. Hague, Kluwer , 1996

Israel's foreign relations; selected documents 1947 -. Medzini, M. Jerusalem, Ministry for Foreign Affairs, 1976-1981

Israel's parliament; the law of the Knesset. Likhovski, E. S. Oxford, Clarendon Pr., 1971

The Knesset; parliament in the Israeli political system. Mahler, G. London, Associated Univ. Pr., 1981

The law of the State of Israel; an introduction. Bin-Nun, A. Jerusalem, R. Mass, 1990 (Translated from the German)

The legal system of Israel. Rev. ed. Baker, H. E. Jerusalem, Israel Univ. Pr., 1968 (Supplements: 1972-1984)

"Legislation & Litigation". Caspi, Z.. Israeli Business Law; an Essential Guide. Ed. by A. Kaplan. Hague, Kluwer, 1996

HUMAN & CIVIL RIGHTS

Combined initial and first periodic report concerning the implementation of the International Covenant on Civil and Political Rights (ICCPR); submitted in 1998 to the United Nations Human Rights Committee. R. D. Bardenstein. Jerusalem, Ministry of Foreign Affairs, Ministry of Justice.

Combined initial and second report of the State of Israel concerning the implementation of the United Nations Covenant on Economic, Social and Cultural Rights (CESCR); submitted in 1997 to the United Nations Committee on Economic, Social and Cultural Rights. United Nations Covenant on Economic, Social and Cultural Rights (CESCR) (1979). Compiled and edited by Michael Atlan. Jerusalem, Ministry of Foreign Affairs, Ministry of Justice, Ministry of Labor and Social Affairs

Combined 7th, 8th and 9th periodic report of Israel concerning the implementation of the International Convention on the Elimination of all Forms of Racial Discrimination (CERD). International Convention on the Elimination of all Forms of Racial Discrimination (1965). Jerusalem, 1997

Commission of Inquiry into the Events at the Refugee Camps in Beirut. Final report. Yitzhak Kahan, Chairman, Aharon Barak, Yona Efrat. Jerusalem, Government Pr., 1983

Free speech and national security. Edited by S. Shetreet. Dordrecht, M. Nijhoff, 1991 (International studies in human rights; 16)

Human rights in the West Bank and Gaza; legacy and politics. Peleg, Ilan. Syracuse Univ. Pr., 1995

Human rights, self-determination and political change in the occupied Palestinian territories. Ed. By S. Bowen. The Hague, M. Nijhoff, 1997

International perspectives on civil justice; essays in honour of Sir Jack I.H.Jacob. Scott, Ian Russell. London, Sweet & Maxwell, 1990 [pp.11-27: Summary judgment proceedings in Israeli law by S. Goldstein]

Legal justice and social change – a philosophy of law. E. Levine. Jerusalem, R.Mass, 1990

Press law in modern democracies; a comparative study. PN. Lahav, editor. New York, Longman, 1985

The protection of minorities and human rights. Ed. Y. Dinstein; associate ed. M. Tabory. The Hague, Nijhoff, 1992.

Religious human rights in global perspective. Ed. by J. Witte, Jr. and J. D.van der Vyver. The Hague, Nijhoff, 1996. [pp.349-389: Religious human rights in the State of Israel by Asher Maoz]

Secrecy and the right to know. Goren,D. Ramat Gan, Turtledove, 1979

INTELLECTUAL PROPERTY

International copyright; law and practice. Nimmer, Melville B. Albany, N.Y., Matthew Bender, 1994. Includes chapter on Israel by J. Weisman

"Law of Intellectual Property". Gabrielli, A. Israeli Business Law; an Essential Guide. Ed. by A. Kaplan. Hague, Kluwer, 1996

Licensing agreements; patents, know-how, trade secrets and software. Edited by Koyo Yelpaala, D.R. Worley, D. Campbell.

Deventer, Kluwer, 1988 [pp 117-174: Israeli law on protections and restrictions of intellectual property transfers: an overview by Z. N. Tamir]

INTERNATIONAL LAW

Consular immunity from judicial process, with particular reference to Israel. Dinstein, Y.. Jerusalem, Institute for Legislative Research and Comparative Law, 1966

"International Law" Lapidoth, R.. The law of Israel: general surveys. Ed. by I. Zamir and S. Colombo. Jerusalem, Hebrew University, 1995

"International Law and the State of Israel". Lerner, N. Introduction to the Law of Israel. Ed. by A. Shapira and K.De-Witt-Arar. Hague, Kluwer, 1995

An international law miscellany. Rosenne, S. Dordrecht, M. Nijhoff, 1996

Studies in international law; with special reference to the Arab-Israeli conflict. Feinberg, N. Jerusalem, Magnes Pr., 1979

ISRAEL -ARAB CONFLICT, PALESTINIANS, ADMINISTERED TERRITORIES

Agreement on the Gaza Strip and the Jericho Area [Cairo, May 4,1994]. Israel. Ministry of Foreign Affairs. Jerusalem, The Ministry, 1994

The Arab boycott of Israel; economic aggression and world reaction. Chill, D. S. New York, Praeger, 1976

The Arab-Israeli accords; legal perspectives. Ed. by E. Cotran and C. Mallat. The Hague, Kluwer, 1996

The Arab-Israel conflict and its resolution; selected documents. Ed. By R. Lapidoth and M. Hirsch. The Hague, Nijhoff, 1992.

The Arab-Israel conflict in international law; a critical analysis of the Colloquium of Arab Jurists in Algiers. Feinberg, N.. Jerusalem, Magnes Pr., 1970

The Arab-Israeli conflict.Ed. by J. Norton Moore. Princeton, N.J., Princeton Univ. Pr., 1975

Eroding the United Nations Charter. Y.Z. Blum. Nijhoff, 1993

From occupation to interim accords; Israel and the Palestinian territories. Shehadeh, R. London, Kluwer Law Int'l., 1997

Human rights in the Israeli-occupied territories 1967-1982. Cohen, Esther R. Manchester, University Pr., 1985

Human rights, self-determination and political change in the occupied territories. Ed. S. Bowen. Hague, Nijhoff, 1997.

Israel, Jordan and the peace process. Y. Lukacs. Syracuse Univ.

Israel, the intifada and the rule of law. Amit-Kohn, Uzi...[et al]. Tel Aviv, Ministry of Defence, 1993

Israel, the West Bank and international law. Gerson, A. London, F.Cass, 1978

Israel and Palestine; assault on the law of nations. Stone, Julius. Baltimore, Johns Hopkins Univ. Pr., 1981

Israel-Palestine Liberation Organization Interim Agreement on the West Bank and the Gaza Strip [Washington, D.C., September 28, 1995]. Together with: Agreement on the temporary international presence in the city of Hebron (TIPH). Jerusalem.

Israeli-Palestinian Interim Agreement on the West Bank and the Gaza Strip; Washington, D.C., September 28, 1995. Jerusalem, 1995

Law and courts in the Israel-held areas . Hebrew University of Jerusalem. Faculty of law, 1970.

Legal dualism: the absorption of the occupied territories into Israel. E. Benvenisti. Westview Pr., 1990

Law reform in the Palestinian territories. R.A. Hamid. Jerusalem, Israel-Palestine Center for research and information, 1996.

The legal status of the Arabs in Israel. Kretzmer, D.. Boulder, Co., Westview Pr., 1990

Military government in the territories administrated by Israel, 1967-1980; the legal aspects. Ed. by M. Shamgar. Jerusalem, Hebrew University. Faculty of Law, 1982

New political entities in public and private international law: with special reference to the Palestinian entity. Ed. A. Shapira and M. Tabory. Kluwer, 1999

Palestine and Israel: a chA.ge to justice. Quigley, J. Duke Univ.. Press, 1990.

Palestinian lawyers and Israeli rule; law and disorder in the West Bank. Bisharat, G. Austin, Univ. of Texas Pr., 1989

Palestine and international law; the legal aspects of the Arab-Israeli

conflict. Cattan, H.. 2d ed. London, Longman, 1976

Protocol Concerning the Redeployment in Hebron; January 17, 1997

Refugees into citizens; Palestinians and the end of the Arab-Israeli conflict; Arzt, D.. New York. Council on Foreign Relations, 1997.

The rule of law in the areas administered by Israel. International Commission of Jurists. Israel National Section. Israel National Section of the International Commission of Jurists, 1981

Secure boundaries and Middle East peace ; in the light of international law and practice. Blum, Y. Jerusalem, The Hebrew University, 1971

Use of force; the practice of states since World War II including the Israel-Arab conflicts. Weisburd, A. University Park, Pa.., Pennsylvania State Univ. Pr., 1997

The West Bank and the rule of law. Shehadeh, R. Geneva, International Commission of Jurists and its West Bank affiliate Law in the Service of Man, 1980

JERUSALEM

"Jerusalem and the peace process; with maps and Oslo documents." Lapidoth, R.. Israel Law Review, vol. 28, pp.402-434, 1994

Jerusalem, city of law and justice. Ed N. Rakover. Jewish Legal Heritage Society, 1998

Jerusalem in America's foreign policy, 1947-1997. S. Slonim. Kluwer, 1998.

The Jerusalem question and its resolution; selected documents. Edited by R. Lapidoth and Moshe Hirsch. Hague, M. Nijhoff, 1994

JEWISH LAW see chapter on Jewish Law

LABOR

Adjudication of interest disputes; the compulsory arbitration model. Raday, F. Jerusalem, Hebrew Univ., 1983

Comparative analysis of attitudes towards mediation in four countries. By J. Krislov and A. Galin. Tel-Aviv, Univ. of Tel-Aviv. Faculty of Management, 1978

International labour standards; the case of freedom to strike. Ben-Israel, R.. Deventer, Kluwer, 1987

"Labour Law". Ben-Israel, R.. Introduction to the Law of Israel. Ed. by A. Shapira and K. DeWitt-Arar. Kluwer, 1995

Public sector labor and employment law. 2d ed. Lefkowitz, Jerome. Albany, N.Y., N.Y State Bar Assoc., 1998

Topics in Israeli labour law. Ed. M. Goldberg, F. Raday. Hebrew Univ., Faculty of Law, 1995.

LEGAL SYSTEM see GOVERNMENT

LEGISLATION see Chapter on Primary Sources – Legislation

MANDATE LAW see Chapter on Pre-State Materials

MILITARY LAW

Military obedience. Keijzer, N. Sijthoff and Noordhoff, 1978

OTTOMAN LAW see Chapter on Pre-State Materials

PUBLIC LAW

Jurisdiction and illegality; a study in public law. Rubinstein,A. Oxford, Clarendon Pr., 1965

Public law in Israel. Itzhak Zamir and A. Zysblat. Oxford, Clarendon Pr., 1996

REAL PROPERTY

Equitable rights to land and the remedy of specific performance of contracts for the sale of land. Doukhan-Landau, L. Jerusalem, Institute for Legislative Research and Comparative Law, 1968

The idea of property in history and modern times. Ed. by C. Kolbert. London, Churchill Pr., 1997

"Law of Real Property". Wiernik, Arie. Israeli Business Law; an Essential Guide. Ed. By A. Kaplan. Hague, Kluwer, 1996

Private property, culture and ideology – Israel's Supreme Court and the jurisprudence of land expropriation. Y. Holzman-Gazit, 1997. Thesis – Ph.D. Stanford Univ.

"Property Law". Deutch, M. Introduction to the Law of Israel. Ed. by A. Shapira and K. DeWitt-Arar. Hague, Kluwer, 1995

"Property Law". Weisman, Joshua. The law of Israel: general surveys. Ed. by I. Zamir and S. Colombo. Jerusalem, Hebrew University, 1995

RELIGION AND STATE

See also Chapter on Jewish Law

Halakhah and mishpat hamelukhah - Jewish law in a civil state. Articles in English and Hebrew. Jewish Political Studies Review, v.10, nos.3/4, 1998.

Perpetual dilemma: Jewish religion in the Jewish state. Abramov, Shene'ur Zalman. Rutherford, N.J., Farleigh Dickinson U.P., 1976

The politics of compromise; state and religion in Israel. Birnbaum, Ervin. Rutherford, N.J., Fairleigh Dickinson U.P., 1970

Religious law in the Israel legal system. Englard, I.. Translated from the Hebrew by M. Losowisk and P. Elman. Jerusalem, Hebrew Univ. of Jerusalem. Faculty of Law, 1975

The rift in Israel; religious authority and secular democracy. L., Samuel. New York, Schocken, 1971

TAXATION

Business operations in Israel. Rafael, Amnon. Washington, D.C., BNA, 1990 (Tax management foreign income portfolios; 417-2nd)

"Double Taxation Relief" Israeli Business Law; an Essential Guide. Ed. by A. Kaplan. Hague, Kluwer, 1996

Evasion and avoidance of income tax; a comparative study of English law and Israeli law. Lapidoth, A. Jerusalem, Museum of Taxes, 1966.

International double taxation. Rafael, Amnon and Efrati, D.. Tel Aviv, Foreign Investors' Organization, Manufacturers Association of Israel, Investment Authority, 1977

International tax summaries – guide for planning and decisions. Coopers & Lybrand. N.Y., Wiley, 1998. Chapter on Israel.

The tax consequences of devaluation: the approach of the Israel law. Neeman, Y.Tel-Aviv, Israel Tax Institute, 1969.

The tax consequences upon conversion of property's use. Neeman, Y. Tel-Aviv, Schocken, 1970

"Tax Law". Hadari, Y. Introduction to the Law of Israel. Ed. by A. Shapira and K. DeWitt-Arar. Hague, Kluwer, 1995

"Taxation of Foreign Residents and Immigrants". Rosenberg, G. Israeli Business Law; an Essential Guide. Ed. by A. Kaplan. Hague, Kluwer, 1996

Taxes and people in Israel. Wilkenfeld, H.C. Cambridge, Mass., Harvard Univ. Pr., 1973.

Transnational taxation of foreign investments in Israel. Klugman, G. Y. Salomon, Lipschutz, 1992

The use of estimation for the assessment of taxable income, with special emphasis on the problems of taxing small business. Lapidoth, A. Amsterdam, International Bureau of Fiscal Documentation, 1977.

TORTS

The law of civil wrongs; general part. Tedeschi, G. Jerusalem, 1969

"Law of Tort". Arbel, D.. Israeli Business Guide; an Essential Guide. Ed. by A. Kaplan. Hague, Kluwer, 1996

"Tort Law". Gilead, Israel. The law of Israel: general surveys. Ed. by I. Zamir and S. Colombo. Jerusalem, Hebrew University, 1995

"Tort Law". Porat, Ariel. Introduction to the Law of Israel.Ed. by A. Shapira. Hague, Kluwer, 1995.

TRUSTS

"Law of Trusts" . Kerem, S. Israeli Business Law; an Essential Guide. Ed. by A. Kaplan. Hague, Kluwer, 1996

WATER

Freedom of navigation with special reference to international waterways in the Middle East. Lapidoth, R.. Jerusalem, Hebrew Univ., 1975 (Jerusalem papers on peace problems; 13,14)

The Jordan River dispute. Saliba, S. Hague, M. Nijhoff, 1968

The Middle Eastern States and the law of the sea. El-Hakim Ali, A. Manchester Univ. Pr., 1979

Water and peace; water resources and the Arab-Israeli peace process. E Kally. Praeger, 1993

WOMEN

Between the flag and the banner; women in Israeli politics. Yishai, Yael. Albany, State University of New York Pr., 1997

Combined initial and second report of the State of Israel concerning the implementation of the United Nations Convention on the Elimination of all Forms of Discrimination against Women (CEDAW); submitted in 1997 to the United Nations Committee on the Elimination of Discrimination against Women. By R. Halperin-Kaddari. Jerusalem,

Ministry of Foreign Affairs, Ministry of Justice.

Women and Islamic law in a non-Muslim state; a study based on decisions of the sharia courts in Israel. Layish, A. New York, Wiley, 1975

Women in Israel. Edited by Y. Azmon, D. N. Izraeli. New Brunswick, Transaction Publ., 1993

MISCELLANEOUS

Inheritance in Israel for the layman and the lawyer. Ed. By J. Harpaz and M. Zaslansky. Haifa Law Publishers, 1990.

International Conference on Equity, Jerusalem. Equity and contemporary legal developments. Ed. Goldstein, S. Hebrew Univ., 1992.

Law and equality in education. Goldstein, S. Jerusalem, Van Leer Jerusalem Foundation, 1980

"Private International Law". Shapira, A. Introduction to the Law of Israel. Ed. by A. Shapira and K. DeWitt-Arar. Hague, Kluwer, 1995

ABBREVIATIONS IN ENGLISH

(Reprinted from World Dictionary of Legal Abbreviations)

A.A. Arbitration Awards. Published by Tribunal for Voluntary Arbitration in the Public Services, 1977 - .

A.D.A. Administrative Detention Appeal.

A.G. Attorney – General.

Adv. Advocate.

A.L.A. Application for Leave to Appeal.

A.L.P. Annotated Laws of Palestine. Edited By A.M. Apelbom. 1944-1948, 6v

A.L.R. Annotated Law Reports, edited by M. Levanon and A.M. Apelbom. 1943-1947.

Bentwich. Legislation of Palestine, 1918-1925. Compiled by Norman Bentwich, 1926. 2v.

C.A. Civil Appeal.

C.C. Civil Case.

C.C.O. Criminal Code Ordinance.

C.L.R. Current Law Reports, edited by M. Levanon. 1937-1942, 11v.

C.O.J. Collection of Judgments, edited by L.M. Rotenberg. 1918-1933, 6v.; 1934-1936, 3v.

C.P.O.A. Collection of Proclamations, Orders and Appointments by the Judea and Samaria Command, Official gazette of the military government.

Cr.A. Criminal Appeal.

Cr.A.D.C. Criminal Appeal in the District Court.

Cr.C.D.C. Criminal Cases in the District Court.

Cr.f. Criminal File.

Ct. Court.

Ct.L.R. Current Law Reports. see C.L.R.

D.H. Divrei HaKnesset, records of the Knesset (Israel legislature) proceedings.

D.I. Dinei Israel – Annual of Jewish Law and Israel Family law, Tel Aviv University, Faculty of Law, 1969-.

D.I. Dinei Israel or Dinei Yisrael. Official revised Hebrew text of pre-State legislation. No.1, 1954 (no.2 and following see D.M.I.)

D.K. Divrei HaKnesset, Records of Knesset (Israel legislature) proceedings, 1949 - .

D.M.I. Dinei Medinat Israel (Nusah Hadash). Official revised Hebrew text of pre-State legislation, new version, no.2 and following. (For no.1, see D.I.).

D.P. Deputy President (Supreme Court).

Drayton. Consolidated edition of pre-State legislation in force in Dec. 31, 1933. Laws of Palestine, edited by R.H. Drayton. 3 v.

E.A. Election Appeal.

F.H. Further Hearing

HaPraklit. Legal periodical published by Israel Bar Association, 1943-

Hatza'ot Hok. (H.H.) Legislative draft bills.

H.C. Petition to the High Court of Equity.

H.H. Hatza'ot Hok – Legislative draft bills.

H.L.R. Haifa Law Reports, 1938-1948.

Hukei Takziv. Budgetary legislation.

I.D.F. Israel Defence Forces.

I.L. Israel pounds (lirot). Currency until September 1980.

I.L.R. Israel Law Review. Quarterly published by Hebrew University, Faculty of Law, 1966 -.

I.N.S. Israel new shekel – currency from January 1986 to date.

I.R. Iton Rishmi. Translation into Hebrew of Palestine Gazette, 1932-1948. Also official gazette during the Provisional Council of State, 1948-1949 ; continued by Reshumot.

I.S. Israel shekel – currency from October 1980 to December 1985.

Is.L.Rev. Israel Law Review, 1966 - .

Isr. Israel.

I.T.O. Income Tax Ordinance.

I.Y.H.R. Israel Yearbook on Human Rights, Tel Aviv University, Faculty of Law 1966 - .

Iyunei Mishpat. Tel Aviv University Law Review, 1971 -

Jdgt. Judgment.

Jm. Jerusalem.

J.P. Justice of the Peace.

K.A. Kitvei Amana. Treaty documents. Section of government gazette, Reshumot.

K.H. Kovetz HaTakanot. Regulations. Section of government gazette, Reshumot.

Kitvei Amana. Treaty documents. Section of government gazette, Reshumot.

Knesset. Israel legislature, unicameral, 120 members.

Kovetz HaTakanot. Regulations. Section of official gazette, Reshumot. Official publication of subsidiary legislation.

K.T. Kovetz HaTakanot. Regulations. Section of government gazette, Reshumot.

Laws of Palestine. Edited by R.H. Drayton, 1934, 3v. Revised edition of consolidated pre-State legislation in force on Dec. 31, 1933.

L.C. Labour Court.

L.C. Land Court (Palestine).

L.S.I. Laws of the State of Israel Authorized English translation of legislative enactments.

L.S.I. (N.V.) Laws of the State of Israel, New Version. Authorized English translation of the revised text of some pre–State legislation.

M. Motion.

M.A. Miscellaneous Applications.

Mag. Magistrate, lower court judge.

M.C. Magistrates Court .

Mehkarei Mishpat. Bar Ilan University Law Review, 1980 - .

Mej. Mejelle. Moslem code of law in force in Ottoman Palestine, and Israel, finally repealed in 1984.

Mishna. Code of ancient Jewish law, edited by Rabbi Judah HaNasi, 200 C.E.

Mishpatim. Hebrew University Law Review, 1970 - .

M.K. Member of Knesset (legislature).

N.L.R. Northern Law Reports, 1938.

N.V. New Version. See: L.S.I. (N.V.)

O. Order

O.C.P.C. Ottoman Civil Procedure Code.

O.L.L. Ottoman Land Law.

O.G. Official Gazette of the Government of Palestine, 1920-1931. Continued by Palestine Gazette, 1932-1948.

Ott. Ottoman.

P. President (Supreme Court).

P.D. Piskei Din. Reports of decisions of the Supreme Court 1948 - .

P.D.A. Piskei Din Avoda. Decisions of the Labour Court, 1969 - .

P.D.E. Piskei Din Ezrahiim . Decisions of the Income Tax Commissioner.

P.D.R. Piskei Din Rabbaniim. Decisions of the Rabbbinical Courts, 1954 - .

P.E. Psakim Elyon. Reports of decisions of the Supreme Court of Israel, 1948-1961,published by Israel Bar Association.

P.G. Palestine Gazette. Government gazette of Mandate Palestine, 1932-1948. Preceded by Official Gazette of the Government of Palestine (O.G.),1920-1931. Supplement 1 includes legislation. Supplement 2 includes regulations.

Piskei Din. (P.D.) Reports of decisions of the Supreme Court, 1948-.

Piskei Din Avoda (P.D.A.) Decisions of the Labour Court, 1969.

Piskei Din Borrerut. Arbitration Awards. Published by Tribunal for Voluntary Arbitration in the Public Services, 1977-.

Piskei Din Ezrahiim. (P.D.E.) Decisions of the Income Tax Commissioner.

Piskei Din Rabbaniim. (P.D.R.) Decisions of the Rabbinical Courts, 1954-.

Piskei Din Refuah u-Mishpat. Law and medicine decisions. Published by Israel Medical Union & Israel Bar Association, 1989-.

Piskei Din Shalom. Magistrates Court decisions. Published by Israel Bar Association, Tel Aviv District, 1988-.

Piskei Din Ta'avura. Transportation decisions. Published by Israel Bar Association, Tel Aviv District, 1985-.

P.L.R. Palestine Law Reports or Law Reports of Palestine. edited by M. McDonnell, 1920-1947.

P.M. Psakim Mehoziim. Reports of decisions of the District Courts, 1949 - . Includes some Magistrates Courts decisions.

P.S. Personal status case.

Psakim. Reports of decisions of the Supreme Court and District Courts, 1948/49. Volume one contains both Supreme and District Court decisions. From volume two the series split into two sets : Supreme Court decisions – Psakim Elyon , and District Court decisions – Psakim Mehoziim.

Psakim Elyon. Reports of decisions of the Supreme Court of Israel, 1948/49 – 1961, Published by the Israel Bar Association.

Psakim Mehoziim. Reports of decisions of the District Courts of Israel, 1948/49 -, published by the Israel Bar Association.

Reshumot. Official government gazette, 1949 - , composed of a number of sections including Sefer HaHukim, Hatza'ot Hok, Kitvei Amana, Kovetz HaTakanot, Yalkut HaPirsumim, Yoman HaPtentim, Yoman Simanei Mishar.

S.C.D.C. Selected Cases of the District Courts, 1943-1947, 5v.

S.C.J. Annotated Supreme Court Judgment, 1939-1942.

S.Ct. Supreme Court.

S.D.C. Selected Cases of the District Courts, 1943-1947, 5v.

Sefer HaHukim. Legislative enactments of the Knesset, 1949 -. Section of the government gazette, Reshumot.

S.H. Sefer HaHukim. Legislative enactments of the Knesset, 1949 - . Section of the government gazette, Reshumot.

Shulhan Arukh. Authoritative code of Jewish law. Edited by Rabbi Joseph Caro, 16th century.

S.J. Selected Judgments of the Supreme Court, 1948 - . Authorized English translation.

S.S.A. State Service Appeal.

S.T. Special Tribunal.

T.A. Tel Aviv

T.A.L.R. Law Reports of the District Court of Tel Aviv, 1937-1938 ; 1941-1942.

T.B. Babylonian Talmud.

Tel Aviv U.L. Rev. Iyunei Mishpat, law review of Tel Aviv University, 1971 - .

T.J. Jerusalem Talmud.

Yad. Yad HaHazaka of Mishneh Torah, Maimonides' code of Jewish law.

Yalkut Hapirsumim. Section of government gazette, Reshumot, containing government notices.

Yoman HaPatentim. Section of government gazette, Reshumot, containing notices of patents.

Yoman Simanei Mishar. Section of government gazette, Reshumot, containing notices of trade marks.

Y.P. Yalkut HaPirsumim. Section of government gazette, Reshumot, containing government notices.

Abbreviations in Hebrew

(transliteration in parentheses)

(Reprinted from World Dictionary of Legal Abbreviations)

Meaning	Abbreviation
Third section of the code of Jewish law, Shulhan Arukh, dealing with civil law matters	(Even ha'ezer) אבה"ע
Others	אחי
Miscellaneous applications	ב"ש
Miscellaneous civil application	בש"א
Miscellaneous criminal application	בש"פ
Petition to the High Court of Justice	(Bagatz) בג"צ
Incorporated	בע"מ
Miscellaneous application to the High Court of Equity	בשג"צ
Petition to the District Court or special court	בד"מ
Application for permission to marry	בה"נ
King's Order-in Council – Mandate Palestine	(D'var hamelekh) דבה"מ
Hearing in the National Labour Court	דב"ע
Additional Hearing	(Diyun nosaf) ד"נ
Records of Knesset – Israel legislature – proceedings, 1949 -.	(Divrei HaKnesset) ד"כ
Opening motion	(Hamratzat p'tiha) ה"פ
Execution of judgment	(Hotza'a lepoal) הוצל"פ
Draft legislative bills	(Hatza'ot hok) ה"ח
Motion	(Hamratza) המי
Draft bills of Hebrew revised text of pre-State legislation	(Hatza'ot nusah hadash) הנ"ח
Decisions of the courts, edited by A.M. Apelbom, 1946-1948, 3v.	(HaMishpat) המשפט
Legal periodical, edited by S. Eisenstadt, 1927.	(HaMishpat) המשפט
And others	ואחי
Fourth section of the code of Jewish law, Shulhan Arukh dealing with civil law matters	(Hoshen Mishpat) הו"מ

Code of Jewish law, 15th century	(Tur) טור
Law, Statute	(Huk) חוק
Attorney – General	(Yoetz Hamishpati) יוהמ"ש
Power of attorney	(Yipui Koah) י"כ
Attorney – General	י"מ
Section of government gazette, containing government notices	(Yalkut HaPirsumim) י"פ
Treaty documents	(Kitvei Amana) כ"א
Retrial	(Mishpat Hozair) מ"ח
Jewish law	(Mishpat Ivri) מ"ע
Decisions of the Rent Tribunal, edited by Meiri	מאירי
Number	מס'
Code of ancient Jewish law edited Rabbi Judah HaNasi, 200 C.E.	(Mishna) משנה
Versus	נ'
New Version. Hebrew revised text of pre-State legislation	(Nusah hadash) נ"ח
Aforementioned	נ"ל
Laws enacted by the Knesset, 1949 – Section of the government gazette, Reshumot.	(Sfer HaHukim) ס"ח
Summaries of Supreme Court decisions edited by Savir	סביר
Civil appeal	(Ir'ur ezrahi) ע"א
Election appeal	(Ir'ur behirot) ע"ב
Lawyer, Advocate	(Orekh din) עו"ד
Page, pages	עמ'
Income tax appeal	(Ir'ur mas hahnasa) עמ"ה
Criminal appeal	(Ir'ur plili) ע"פ
Official Gazette – pre-State	(Iton Rishmi) ע"ר
Official Gazette. Supplement one – contains ordinances	ע"ר תוס' 1
Local Authority appeal	(Ir'ur reshut mekomi) ער"מ

Miscellaneous appeals	(Ir'urim shonim) ע"ש
Decisions of the Supreme Court	(Piskei Din) פ"ד
Decisions of the Income Tax Commissioner	(Piskei Din Ezrahiim) פד"א
Decisions of the Supreme Court	(Piskei Din) פד"י
Decisions of the Labour Court	(Piskei Din Avoda) פד"ע
Decisions of the Rabbinical Court	(Piskei Din Rabbaniim) פד"ר
Decisions of the District Court. Includes also some Magistrate Court decisions	(Piskei Din Mehoziim) פ"מ
Summaries of decisions of the District Courts; appear at end of volume	(ת) פ"מ
Decisions, report, judgment	(Psak Din) פס"ד
Decisions of the District Court	(Psakim Mehoziim) פס"מ
Court decisions	(Piskei Din) פסקי דין
Arbitration Awards. Published by Tribunal for Voluntary Arbitration in the Public Services, 1977-	פסקי דין בוררות (Piskei Din Borerrut)
Magistrates' Court decisions. Published by Israel Bar Association, Tel Aviv District, 1988-.	פסקי דין בתי משפט שלום (Piskei Din Shalom)
Law and medicine decisions. Published by Israel Medical Union and Israel Bar Association, 1989- .	פסקי דין רפואה ומשפט (Piskei Din Refuah u-Mishpat)
Transportation decisions	פסקי דין תעבורה (Piskei Din Ta'avura)
Decisions of the Supreme Court, published by Israel Bar Association, 1948-1961.	(Psakim Elyon) פ"ע
Ordinance. Pre-State statute	(P'kuda) פק'
Decisions of the Magistrates' Courts	פ"ש
Israel Defence Forces	(Tzahal) צה"ל
Regulations. Section of the government gazette, Reshumot.	(Kovetz HaTakanot) ק"ת
Regulations covering customs and purchase tax	ק"ת שעורי מק"ח (Kovetz HaTakanot)
Journal of Accountancy	(Roeh HaHeshbon) רו"ח
Maimonides. Usually refers to his 14 volume work of Jewish law "Mishneh Torah" also known	(Rambam) רמב"ם

as “Yad Hahazaka”, 12th century

Allowance to appeal (Reshut ir'ur) ר"ע
Allowance to civil appeal רע"א
Allowance to criminal appeal רע"פ

Authoritative code of Jewish law
edited by Rabbi Joseph Caro, 16th century. (Shulhan Arukh) שו"ע

Responsa literature (Sh’elot u'Teshuvot) שו"ת

Civil case (Tik ezrahi) ת"א
Guardianship case תא"פ
Elections to Knesset case תב"כ

Labour court case תב"ע

Supplement (Tosefet) תוס'

Personal status case תמ"א

Bible (Tanah) תנ"ך

Criminal case (Tik plili) ת"פ

Estate case ת"ע
Will case ת"צ

Rule, regulation (Takana) תק'

DECLARATION OF THE ESTABLISHMENT OF THE STATE OF ISRAEL

ERETZ-ISRAEL[1] was the birthplace of the Jewish people. Here their spiritual, religious and political identity was shaped. Here they first attained to statehood, created cultural values of national and universal significance and gave to the world the eternal Book of Books.

After being forcibly exiled from their land, the people kept faith with it throughout their Dispersion and never ceased to pray and hope for their return to it and for the restoration in it of their political freedom.

Impelled by this historic and traditional attachment, Jews strove in every successive generation to re-establish themselves in their ancient homeland. In recent decades they returned in their masses. Pioneers, ma'pilim[2] and defenders, they made the deserts bloom, revived the Hebrew language, built villages and towns, and created a thriving community, controlling its own economy and culture, loving peace but knowing how to defend itself, bringing the blessings of progress to all the country's inhabitants, and aspiring towards independent nationhood.

In the year 5657 (1897), at the summons of the spiritual father of the Jewish State, Theodore Herzl, the First Zionist Congress convened and proclaimed the right of the Jewish people to national rebirth in its own country.

This right was recognised in the Balfour Declaration of the 2nd November, 1917, and re-affirmed in the Mandate of the League of Nations which, in particular, gave international sanction to the historic connection between the Jewish people and Eretz-Israel and to the right of the Jewish people to rebuild its National Home.

The catastrophe which recently befell the Jewish people – the massacre of millions of Jews in Europe – was another clear demonstration of the urgency of solving the problem of its homelessness by re-establishing in Eretz-Israel the Jewish State, which would open the gates to the homeland wide to every Jew and confer upon the Jewish people the status of a fully-privileged member of the comity of nations.

Survivors of the Nazi holocaust in Europe, as well as Jews from other parts of the world, continued to migrate to Eretz-Israel, undaunted by difficulties, restrictions and dangers, and never ceased to assert their right to a life of dignity, freedom and honest toil in their national homeland.

In the Second World War, the Jewish community of this country contributed its full share to the struggle of the freedom-and peace-loving nations against the forces of Nazi wickedness and, by the blood of its

---

[1] Eretz-Israel (Hebrew) – the Land of Israel, Palestine.

[2] Ma'pilim (Hebrew) – immigrants coming to Eretz-Israel in defiance of restrictive legislation

soldiers and its war effort, gained the right to be reckoned among the peoples who founded the United Nations.

On the 29th November, 1947, the United Nations General Assembly passed a resolution calling for the establishment of a Jewish State in Eretz-Israel; the General Assembly required the inhabitants of Eretz-Israel to take such steps as were necessary on their part for the implementation of that resolution. This recognition by the United Nations of the right of the Jewish people to establish their State is irrevocable.

This right is the natural right of the Jewish people to be masters of their own fate, like all other nations, in their own sovereign State.

ACCORDINGLY WE, MEMBERS OF THE PEOPLE'S COUNCIL, REPRESENTATIVES OF THE JEWISH COMMUNITY OF ERETZ-ISRAEL, AND OF THE ZIONIST MOVEMENT, ARE HERE ASSEMBLED ON THE DAY OF THE TERMINATION OF THE BRITISH MANDATE OVER ERETZ-ISRAEL, AND, BY VIRTUE OF OUR NATURAL AND HISTORIC RIGHT AND ON THE STRENGTH OF THE RESOLUTION OF THE UNITED NATIONS GENERAL ASSEMBLY, HEREBY DECLARE THE ESTABLISHMENT OF A JEWISH STATE IN ERETZ-ISRAEL, TO BE KNOWN AS THE STATE OF ISRAEL.

WE DECLARE that, with effect from the moment of the termination of the Mandate, being tonight, the eve of Sabbath, the 6th Iyar, 5708 (15th May, 1948), until the establishment of the elected, regular authorities of the State in accordance with the Constitution which shall be adopted by the Elected Constituent Assembly not later than the 1st October 1948, the People's Council shall act as a Provisional Council of State, and its executive organ, the People's Administration, shall be the Provisional Government of the Jewish State, to be called "Israel".

THE STATE OF ISRAEL will be open for Jewish immigration and for the Ingathering of the Exiles; it will foster the development of the country for the benefit of all its inhabitants; it will be based on freedom, justice and peace as envisaged by the prophets of Israel; it will ensure complete equality of social and political rights to all its inhabitants irrespective of religion, race or sex; it will guarantee freedom of religion, conscience, language, education and culture; it will safeguard the Holy Places of all religions; and it will be faithful to the principles of the Charter of the United Nations.

THE STATE OF ISRAEL is prepared to cooperate with the agencies and representatives of the United Nations in implementing the resolution of the General Assembly of the 29th November, 1947, and will take steps to bring about the economic union of the whole of Eretz-Israel.

WE APPEAL to the United Nations to assist the Jewish people in the building-up of its State and to receive the State of Israel into the comity of nations.

WE APPEAL – in the very midst of the onslaught launched against us now for months – to the Arab inhabitants of the State of Israel to preserve peace and participate in the upbuilding of the State on the basis of full and equal citizenship and due representation in all its provisional and permanent institutions.

WE EXTEND our hand to all neighbouring states and their peoples in an offer of peace and good neighbourliness, and appeal to them to establish bonds of cooperation and mutual help with the sovereign Jewish people settled in its own land. The State of Israel is prepared to do its share in a common effort for the advancement of the entire Middle East.

WE APPEAL to the Jewish people throughout the Diaspora to rally round the Jews of Eretz-Israel in the tasks of immigration and upbuilding and to stand by them in the great struggle for the realization of the age-old dream – the redemption of Israel.

PLACING OUR TRUST IN THE ALMIGHTY, WE AFFIX OUR SIGNATURES TO THIS PROCLAMATION AT THIS SESSION OF THE PROVISIONAL COUNCIL OF STATE, ON THE SOIL OF THE HOMELAND, IN THE CITY OF TEL-AVIV, ON THIS SABBATH EVE, THE 5TH DAY OF IYAR, 5708 (14TH May, 1948).

David Ben-Gurion

Daniel Auster
Mordekhai Bentov
Yitzchak Ben Zvi
Eliyahu Berligne
Fritz Bernstein
Rabbi Wof Gold
Meir Grabovsky
Yitzchak Gruenbaum
Dr. Abraham Granovsky

Eliyahu Dobkin
Meil Wilner-Kovner
Zerach Wahrhaftig
Herzl Vardi
Rachel Cohen
Rabbi Kalman Kahana
Saadia Kobashi
Rabbi Yitzchak Meir Levin
Meir David Loewenstein
Zvi Luria
Golda Myerson
Nachum Nir
Zvi Segal
Rabbi Yehuda Leib Hacohen Fishman
David Zvi Pinkas
Aharon Zisling
Moshe Kolodny
Eliezer Kaplan
Abraham Katznelson
Felix Rosenblueth
David Remez
Berl Repetur
Mordekhai Shattner
Ben Zion Sternberg
Bekhor Shitreet
Moshe Shapira
Moshe Shertok

PROCLAMATION

In virtue of the Declaration of Independence published this day, the fifth of Iyar, five thousand seven hundred and eight (14th May, 1948), under which the Provisional Council of State and the Provisional Government of the State of Israel have been constituted, the Provisional Council of State hereby declares as follows:

1. The Provisional Council of State is the legislative authority. The Provisional Council of State is entitled to delegate some of its

legislative power to the Provisional Government for the purpose of urgent legislation.

2. Such provisions of the law as arise from the White Paper of 1939 are hereby declared null and void.
   Sections 13 to 15 of the Immigration Ordinance, 1941, and Regulations 102 to 107C of the Defence (Emergency) Regulations, 1945, are hereby repealed.
   The Land Transfers Regulations, 1940, are hereby repealed retroactively as from the 29th Iyar, 5699 (18th May, 1939).

3. So long as no laws have been enacted by or on behalf of the Provisional Council of State, the law which existed in Palestine on the 5th Iyar, 5708 (14th May, 1948) shall continue in force in the State of Israel, in so far as such continuance in force is consistent with the contents of this Proclamation, with the future laws and with the changes arising from the establishment of the State and its authorities.

Given this day, the 5th Iyar, 5708 (14th May, 1948).

THE PROVISIONAL COUNCIL OF STATE

Published in the Official Gazette, no.1 of the 5th Iyar, 5708 (14th May, 1948); 1 L.S.I.3-6, 1948

INDEX